S0-BAD-457

KEY WORDS for Better Understanding China

Compiled by
Guo Yakun, Tian Jie, Ma Yanrong

Translated by
Li Yang, Wang Qin, Feng Xin, Qu Lei,
Zhou Xiaogang, Yan Jing

Foreign Languages Press

First Edition 2008

ISBN 978-7-119-05347-9

Published by Foreign Languages Press
24 Baiwanzhuang Road, Beijing 100037, China
http://www.flp.com.cn

Distributed by China International Book Trading Corporation
35 Chegongzhuang Xilu, Beijing 100044, China
P.O. Box 399, Beijing, China

Printed in the People's Republic of China

Contents

Foreword

Over the past decade, China's economy has kept up a swift and steady pace of growth, and China's market potential is still expanding.

Along with the accelerating trend toward globalization, enterprises from all over the world are flocking to invest in China. It has therefore become imperative for their business strategies that they obtain a better comprehension of China as well as a mutual understanding with their Chinese partners, to ensure the success of their ventures.

This book contains over 200 key words and phrases which are directly related to the politics, economy, society, culture, science and technology, environmental protection and other fields which are part and parcel of modern China. The book is designed to help the reader obtain a more accurate grasp of the reality of China in its latest rapid modernization phase.

政治

Politics

改革开放

Reform and Opening-up

China's reform and opening-up policy was introduced at the Third Plenum of the 11th Central Committee of the Communist Party of China in 1978. Over the years, reform has spread from the countryside to the cities, from the economic system to other systems, and opening-up has moved from revitalizing the domestic economy to opening up to the outside world. Reform and opening-up has now become a basic State policy of China.

Reform first commenced in the rural areas in 1979, when the people's communes, integrating government administration with commune management, was replaced by the household contract responsibility system, linking remuneration to output. Farmers regained the right to use land and to arrange their farm work and dispose of farm produce. Reform shifted from the countryside to the cities in 1984, with the decision-making power of enterprises expanding and the economic administrative function of the government transformed. At the same time, reform of the political, cultural, scientific and technological, and educational systems got started. In 1992, after a dozen or so years of experiment, China finally set the socialist market economy as the goal of its reform. In accordance with the plan, a relatively sound socialist market economy will be established by 2010, and by 2020 the socialist market economy will have a comparatively mature structure.

As urban and rural reform progresses, China is implementing the opening-up strategy in planned and step-by-step way. Since 1980, five special economic zones have been set up—in Shenzhen, Zhuhai and Shantou in Guangdong Province, Xiamen in Fujian Province, and Hainan Province, respectively. In 1984, China further opened 14 coastal cities—Dalian, Qinhuangdao,

Tianjin, Yantai, Qingdao, Lianyungang, Nantong, Shanghai, Ningbo, Wenzhou, Fuzhou, Guangzhou, Zhanjiang and Beihai. Then, beginning in 1985, the Yangtze River Delta, Pearl River Delta, Xiamen-Zhangzhou-Quanzhou Triangle in southern Fujian, Shandong Peninsula, Liaodong Peninsula, Hebei Province and the Guangxi Zhuang Autonomous Region were opened up and formed an open coastal belt. In 1990, the Chinese government decided to develop and open the Pudong New Zone in Shanghai, and opened more cities along the Yangtze River. In this way, a chain of open cities extending up the Yangtze River valley, with Pudong at the head, took shape. Since 1992, the Chinese government has opened a number of border cities, and all the capital cities of inland provinces and autonomous regions. In addition, 15 free trade zones, 54 State-level economic and technological development zones, and 53 new- and high-tech industrial development zones have been established in large and medium-sized cities. As a result, a multi-level, omni-directional and multi-channel pattern of opening-up, integrating coastal areas with riverine, border and inland areas, has been formed in China. As these open areas adopt different preferential policies, they play the dual role of "windows" in developing the foreign-oriented economy, generating foreign exchange through exporting products and importing advanced technology, and of "radiators" in accelerating inland economic development.

两会

NPC and CPPCC

The NPC and CPPCC refer to the National People's Congress and Chinese People's Political Consultative Conference, respectively. Each member of the NPC Standing Committee and

CPPCC National Committee serves a term of five years. Both committees meet annually, usually in the first quarter of the year.

The NPC, the highest organ of State power of the People's Republic of China (PRC), is composed of representatives selected by provinces, autonomous regions, municipalities directly under the central government, special administrative regions and military units. It exercises legislative power, and decides on key issues of political life. The NPC has the power to amend the Constitution and supervise its enforcement; enact and amend criminal, civil, State-institutional and other basic laws; examine and approve the plan for national economic and social development and the State budget, and report on their implementation; approve the establishment of provinces, autonomous regions and municipalities directly under the central government; decide on the establishment of special administrative regions and the systems to be instituted within them; decide on questions of war and peace; elect and remove the leaders of the highest State organs, i.e. members of the NPC Standing Committee, president and vice-president of the PRC, premier of the State Council and other State Council members, chairman of the Central Military Commission (CMC) and other CMC members, president of the Supreme People's Court, and procurator-general of the Supreme People's Procuratorate. When the NPC is not in session, its Standing Committee exercises supreme State power.

The CPPCC is neither a State organ nor an ordinary mass organization; rather it is a widely representative, patriotic united front organization of the Chinese people. The CPPCC National Committee consists of representatives of the CPC, non-communist parties, unaffiliated individuals, people's organizations, ethnic minorities and other social strata, compatriots from Taiwan, Hong Kong and Macao, returned overseas

Chinese, and specially invited individuals. The Committee members may attend the National People's Congress meetings as non-voting delegates to practice political consultation and democratic supervision, and participate in the deliberation and administration of State affairs. When the CPPCC is not in session, the Committee organizes its members to conduct specialized activities or make inspection tours to all parts of the country, hold discussions on key issues concerning major State policies, the people's life and the united front, and exercise democratic supervision of the work of State organs and the implementation of the Constitution and State laws through proffering views, suggestions and criticisms.

人民代表大会制度

People's Congress System

The Fifth session of the Tenth National People's Congress was held in Beijing from March 5 to 16, 2007. The picture shows a meeting of the congress.

In China, all power belongs to the people. The organs through which the people exercise State power are the National People's Congress (NPC) and the local people's congresses at various levels. The people's congress system is China's fundamental political system. Its basic characteristics are: It has extensive representation, and is the basic form for the people to administer the country; it follows the principle of democratic centralism, i.e. it guarantees that the people enjoy extensive democracy and rights, at the same time guaranteeing that State power is exercised in a centralized and unified way on the premise that the people's congresses exercise the State power in a unified way. The State's administrative power, judicial authority, procuratorial authority and leadership over the armed forces are clearly divided to ensure that the organs of State power and administrative, judicial, procuratorial and other State organs work in a coordinated way.

Deputies to the people's congresses at all levels are elected, and are responsible to and accept supervision by the people. The deputies are broadly representative; they include people from all ethnic groups, all walks of life, and all regions, classes and strata. When the congresses meet, they can air their views fully or make proposals for addressing inquiries to the people's governments and governmental departments at the corresponding levels. The recipients of such inquiries are bound to reply to them. The voters or the electoral units have the right to recall, in accordance with the law, the deputies they elect.

多党合作和政治协商制度

System of Multi-party Cooperation and Political Consultation

China is a multi-national and multi-party country. As the ruling party, the CPC conducts consultations with all ethnic groups, all non-communist parties, people from all walks of life and unaffiliated individuals on major State policies and matters concerning the national economy and the people's livelihood before decisions are made. This is what is usually called the system of multi-party cooperation and political consultation under the leadership of the CPC, which is the country's basic political system.

In China, besides the CPC, there are eight other political parties: the Revolutionary Committee of the Chinese Kuomintang, China Democratic League, China National Democratic Construction Association, China Association for Promoting Democracy, Chinese Peasants and Workers Democratic Party, China Zhi Gong Dang, Jiu San Society and Taiwan Democratic Self-Government League. They are participating parties rather than opposition parties. They support the CPC leadership politically, which was the historic choice they made during the long years when they cooperated and fought side by side with the CPC for the liberation of the country. These parties enjoy political freedom, organizational independence and lawful equality within the scope of the Constitution. The basic principle of cooperation between the CPC and the other parties is long-term co-existence, mutual supervision, sincere cooperation and the sharing of weal and woe.

和平发展

Peace and Development

For thousands of years, "nothing is more precious than peace" has been the ideological theme of Chinese society. "Do not impose on others what you would not like others to impose on you" is a basic value orientation of the Chinese nation; and "Harmony with differences" and "Great virtue perfects all things" demonstrate the broad-mindedness of the Chinese people. For many years, China has consistently followed an independent foreign policy of peace, the purpose of which is to safeguard world peace and promote common development. As early as in 1974, when he led the Chinese delegation to attend the 6th Special Session of the United Nations, Deng Xiaoping, a brilliant leader in the shaping of modern China, proclaimed to the world that China would never seek hegemony. Since the policies of reform and opening-up were introduced, China, keeping in view the changes in the international situation, has upheld the important strategic judgment that peace and development are the theme of the present times, and stated on many occasions that China did not seek hegemony in the past, nor does it now, and nor will it in the future when it gets stronger. China's development will never pose a threat to other countries; instead, it can bring more development opportunities and bigger markets for the rest of the world. Facts prove that China's economic development is becoming an important impetus for economic growth in the Asia-Pacific region and even the world as a whole. It has become the national determination of China to safeguard world peace and promote common development.

China's intentions in taking the road of peaceful development are to take advantage of the favorable conditions presented by world peace to develop itself and better safeguard and promote world peace through its own development; to base its development mainly on its own resources and its own restructuring and innovation efforts, while also taking an active part in economic globalization and regional cooperation; to continue the process of opening-up and promote cooperation with all other countries on the basis of equality and mutual benefit, concentrate on development and work to preserve a long-term peaceful international environment and an excellent neighboring environment; to never seek hegemony and always remain a staunch force in safeguarding world peace and promoting common development. In short, in taking this road, China pursues development which is peaceful, open, cooperative and harmonious in nature.

三个代表

The Three Represents

The doctrine of the Three Represents, i.e. (the CPC) must always represent the development trend of China's advanced productive forces, the orientation of China's advanced culture and the fundamental interests of the overwhelming majority of the Chinese people, was put forward by Jiang Zemin, former Chinese President and General Secretary of the CPC Central Committee, during his inspection of Guangdong Province in south China in February 2000. The Amendment to the Constitution adopted at the 16th National Congress of the CPC in November 2002 established the Three Represents along with Marxism-Leninism, Mao Zedong Thought and Deng Xiaoping Theory as the guiding ideology that the Party must uphold for a long time to come.

In order to always represent the development trend of China's advanced productive forces, it is necessary to bring the Party's theory, line, program, principles, policies and all its work into line with the law governing the development of the productive forces, give expression to what is required in promoting the liberation and development of social productive forces, especially in the development of advanced productive forces, so that the living standards of the people improve steadily through the development of the productive forces. To ensure that the Party permanently represents the orientation of China's advanced culture, it is imperative that the Party's theory, line, program, principles, policies and all its work should be oriented toward modernization, the world and the future, reflect the requirements of the development of a national, scientific and popular socialist culture, serve to upgrade the ideological and ethical standards and scientific and cultural levels of the whole nation, and provide spiritual and intellectual support for China's economic development and social progress. To guarantee that the Party always represents the fundamental interests of the overwhelming majority of the Chinese people, the Party must, in its theory, line, program, principles, policies and all its work, take the fundamental interests of the people as the starting point and purpose, bring into full play the people's enthusiasm, initiative and creativity, and ensure that the people continue to reap tangible economic, political and cultural benefits on the basis of steady social development and progress.

科学发展观

Scientific Outlook on Development

In October 2003 the scientific outlook on development was established at the Third Plenum of the 16th Central Committee of the CPC. On January 27, 2004 Hu Jintao, Chinese President and General Secretary of the CPC Central Committee, made a statement of the full content of the scientific outlook on development. That is, to put people first, aim at comprehensive, balanced and sustainable development, work to strike a proper balance between urban and rural development, development among regions, economic and social development, development of man and nature, and domestic development and opening-up to the outside world, continue to develop the socialist market economy, political democracy and advanced culture, and promote all-round economic, social, and personal development. Putting people first is the essence and core of the scientific outlook on development.

The Outline of the 11th Five-Year Plan for the National Economic and Social Development of China (2006-2010) calls for comprehensively implementing the scientific outlook on development, and incorporating this outlook into the whole course and every aspect of economic and social development. This will be achieved by building a new socialist countryside, optimizing and upgrading the industrial structure, accelerating the development of the service industry, promoting balanced development among regions, building a resource-conserving and environmental-friendly society, implementing the strategy of developing China through science and education and the strategy of strengthening the country through tapping human resources, deepening institutional reform, further carrying out the opening-up strategy featuring mutual benefit, building a harmonious socialist society, promoting socialist political democracy, promoting socialist cultural development, strengthening national defense and building of the armed forces, and establishing and improving the implementation mechanism of the plan.

以人为本

Putting People First

Hu Jintao, Chinese President and General Secretary of the CPC Central Committee, remarked at the National Symposium on Population, Resources and Environment in March 2004 that putting people first requires the country to set all-round personal development as its target, make the fundamental interests of the broadest masses of the people the point of departure for seeking and promoting development, endeavor to satisfy the people's growing material and cultural needs, and guarantee the economic, political and cultural rights and interests of the general public to let everyone share the benefits of the country's development.

The Outline of the 11th Five-Year Plan has shifted the emphasis on the growth of material wealth to personal development as its point of departure. The Plan, instead of setting the growth of Gross Domestic Product (GDP) as the only criterion for development like before, puts all-round personal development at the core, lists the development of human resources as a key measure, stresses the augmentation of employment, strengthening of compulsory education, and public health and security, and completion of social security coverage, pays more attention to underdeveloped areas and disadvantaged groups, and incorporates humanity and social indicators. According to the National Bureau of Statistics, China will add a number of new indicators, such as happiness, all-round personal development, regional innovation and social harmony, to its statistical items, so as to adapt to the requirements of balanced development of the economy and society, all-round personal development, people's livelihood and humanity. The concept of putting people first not only has a profound influence on the performance, interest and position values of governments at all levels, it also gives rise to wide-ranging changes in all aspects of social life.

和谐社会
Harmonious Society

The 16th National Congress of the CPC in November 2002

put forward "making society more harmonious" as one of the goals of building a moderately prosperous society in all aspects. In September 2004, the Fourth Plenum of the 16th Central Committee of the CPC clearly stated "Enhancing the capacity for constructing a harmonious socialist society" as a key aspect for building the CPC's ruling capacity. A harmonious socialist society pursues democracy and the rule of law, equity and justice, faithfulness and fraternity, and features vigor, stability, orderliness, and harmony between man and Nature.

Statistics show that China's ratio of per capita annual net income of rural residents to per capita disposable income of urban residents grew from 1:2.57 in 1985 to 1:3.23 in 2004, and the ratio of per capita gross income between rural and urban areas was nearly 1:5 in 2004. The great gap between rural and urban areas in educational resources severely hampers the development of countryside. At present, the income gap among China's industries and regions tends to widen. The ratio between the maximum and minimum average pay rose from 2.62:1 in 2000 to 3.98:1 in 2003 and reached 4.25:1 in 2004. The Outline of the 11th Five-Year Plan calls for more attention to social equity, especially in school enrolment, employment and distribution, and for prioritized efforts to raise low incomes, gradually increase middle incomes and effectively adjust exorbitant incomes.

The Resolution of the CPC Central Committee on Major Issues Concerning the Building of a Harmonious Socialist Society adopted at the Sixth Plenum of the 16th Central Committee of the CPC in October 2006 puts forward the main objectives and tasks for building a harmonious socialist society by 2020. They are as follows:

- Further improving the socialist democratic and legal system, implementing in an all-round way the fundamental principle of administering the country in accordance with the law;

respecting and guaranteeing people's rights and interests;

● Gradually reversing the widening gap between urban and rural development, and development between different regions, shape a rational and orderly income distribution pattern, universally increasing household wealth and enabling people to lead more affluent lives;

● Raising the employment rate to a relatively high level, and establishing a social security system covering both urban and rural residents;

● Further improving the basic public services system and significantly raising government administrative and service levels;

● Markedly enhancing the ideological and moral qualities, scientific and cultural qualities and health status of the whole nation, making greater progress in fostering a sound moral atmosphere and harmonious interpersonal relationships;

● Notably reinforcing the creativity of the whole society and constructing an innovational country;

● Perfecting the social administration system and achieving good social order;

● Achieving visible improvement in resources utilization efficiency and the ecological environment; and

● Realizing the objective of building a moderately prosperous society of a higher level and in an all-around way to benefit the more than one billion Chinese people; striving to attain a situation in which all people do their best in accordance with their abilities, everyone being provided for and living together in harmony.

八荣八耻

Eight Honors and Eight Dishonors

The concept of Eight Honors and Eight Dishonors was put

forth by Hu Jintao, Chinese President and General Secretary of the CPC Central Committee, in his speech on the socialist values of honor and dishonor at the joint meeting of the China Democratic League (CDL) and China Association for Promoting Democracy (CAPD) during the Fourth Session of the 10th National Committee of the Chinese People's Political Consultative Conference on March 4, 2006. The content of the Eight Honors and Eight Dishonors is: Love the country, do it no harm. Serve the people, never betray them. Follow science, discard superstition. Be diligent, not indolent. Be united, make no gains at others' expense. Be honest, do not sacrifice ethics for profit. Be disciplined and law-abiding, not chaotic and lawless. Live plainly, work hard, do not wallow in luxuries and pleasures.

The Eight Honors and Eight Dishonors, clearly differentiating good and evil, right and wrong, what to uphold and what to oppose, what to advocate and what to resist, is a guideline conducive to carrying forward and popularizing traditional Chinese virtues; embodies the content of socialist advanced culture; helps bring culture's role in enlightening thought, refining sentiment, imparting knowledge and instilling inspiration into full play; promotes basic socialist ethics and fosters the formation and development of good atmosphere of social ethics; and provides young people with a new creed for life, prompting them to have a correct view of the socialist values of honor and dishonor.

一国两制

One Country, Two Systems

"One country, two systems" is an idea proposed by Deng Xiaoping for solving problems of national unity, and has become a basic State policy of China for realizing reunification. The idea suggests that on the premise of one China, the mainland of China shall continue its socialist system, and the capitalist systems of Hong Kong, Macao and Taiwan shall remain unchanged for a long time to come. The policy of "one country, two systems" has been practiced successfully in Hong Kong and Macao, and will no doubt resolve the Taiwan question and bring about complete national reunification.

The idea of "one country, two systems" and putting it into practice is an ingenious invention of Chinese political wisdom, and is of great domestic and international significance. Firstly, it helps advance China's peaceful reunification cause, which is the common wish of the people of the mainland and Taiwan and the common request of the people of Hong Kong and Macao and overseas Chinese. China's peaceful reunification accords with the trend of the times and the will of the people. Secondly, it facilitates China's modernization and the stability and prosperity of Hong Kong, Macao and Taiwan. The idea not only boosts the implementation of the policy of reform and opening-up on the mainland, but also retains and develops the status and role of Hong Kong, Macao and Taiwan. Thirdly, it contributes to world peace. The idea blazes a new path for settling questions left over from history among countries and international disputes, and provides instructive inspiration for solving certain conflicts and disputes in today's world.

九二共识

1992 Consensus

In November 1992 the mainland's Association for Relations Across the Taiwan Straits (ARATS) and the Straits Exchanges

Foundation (SEF) of Taiwan reached an informal agreement that "the two sides of the Straits adhere to the one-China principle." The agreement is called the 1992 Consensus.

At the end of 1987, the over-30-year isolation between the two sides of the Taiwan Straits finally ended. Economic and cultural exchanges between people of the two sides of the Straits began to increase, but also gave rise to various problems. To solve these problems, the Taiwan authorities had to adjust their policy of "no contact, no concession and no negotiation," and established the SEF, a non-governmental agency, in November 1990 to contact and negotiate with the Chinese mainland. The SEF would, on behalf of the Taiwan authorities, deal with cross-Straits issues, which are "inconvenient or impossible for the Taiwan authorities to handle." To facilitate contact and negotiation with the SEF, the Taiwan Affairs Office of the CPC Central Committee and the Taiwan Affairs Office of the State Council set up the ARATS in December 1991 and authorized it to conduct contacts and businesslike negotiations concerning cross-Straits affairs with the SEF on the "one-China" principle. Since the 1992 Consensus was reached, the ARATS and the SEF have properly handled issues involving the rights and interests of the people on both sides of the Straits, and engaged in businesslike negotiations. In April 1993 successful talks were held between Wang Daohan, chairman of the ARATS, and Koo Chen-fu, chairman of the SEF, in Singapore, and several agreements concerning and protecting the legitimate rights of compatriots on both sides of the Straits were signed. The Talks marked historic progress in cross-Straits relations. In October 1998 Koo Chen-fu visited Shanghai and Beijing, and met Wang Daohan. The two reached four items of common understandings including the implementation of political and economic dialogue between the ARATS and the SEF.

两岸“三通”
“Three Direct Links” across the Taiwan Straits

Shanghai Airlines' flight FM808, the last charter flight for Taiwan businesspeople during the Spring Festival 2005, arrived at Pudong International Airport on February 17, 2005.

On New Year's Day 1979, the Standing Committee of the National People's Congress (NPC) of China issued the Message to Compatriots in Taiwan, initiating the proposal of peaceful reunification. The message expressed the hope that "sooner rather than later transportation and postal services between both sides will be established to make it easier for compatriots of both sides to have direct contact, write to each other, visit relatives and friends, exchange tours and visits, and carry out academic, cultural, sports and technological exchanges." In September 1981, Ye Jianying, then Chairman of the NPC Standing Committee, in a interview with Xinhua News Agency, elaborated on a series of key policies of the Party and the Chinese government concerning peaceful reunification and cross-Straits contacts. Mr. Ye reiterated the proposal that "the two sides make arrangements to facilitate the exchange of mails, trade, air and shipping services, family reunions, and visits by relatives and tourists, as well as academic, cultural and sports exchanges, and reach an agreement thereon." This was the first time the concept and content of the "three direct links" had been made clear, namely postal services, transportation and trade between the mainland of China and Taiwan.

The "three links" were basically realized in an indirect way by the end of the 1980s. "Direct links," with direct shipping and flight at the core, are still unavailable.

和平共处五项原则

Five Principles of Peaceful Coexistence

The Five Principles of Peaceful Coexistence are mutual respect for sovereignty and territorial integrity, mutual non-aggression, non-interference in each other's internal affairs, equality and mutual benefit, and peaceful coexistence. From December 1953 to April 1954, delegations of the Chinese and Indian governments held negotiations in Beijing on their bilateral relations in the Tibet Autonomous Region. The Five Principles were first set forth by Chinese Premier Zhou Enlai to the Indian delegation at the start of the negotiations. Later, they were formally written into the preface to the Agreement between the People's Republic of China and the Republic of India on Trade and Exchanges between the Tibetan Region of China and India. Since June 1954, when the Five Principles were included in the joint communiqué issued by Chinese Premier Zhou Enlai and Indian Prime Minister Jawaharlal Nehru, they have been adopted in many other international documents, and have become widely accepted as norms for relations between countries.

Over the decades the Five Principles have withstood the test of international changes, exhibited dynamism, and played an enormous role in promoting world peace and international friendly cooperation. China is not only a strong proponent but also a faithful practitioner of the Five Principles. On the basis of the Five Principles, China has settled boundary issues left over from history with most of its neighboring countries and established diplomatic ties with over 160 countries.

上海合作组织
Shanghai Cooperation Organization

The Shanghai Cooperation Organization (SCO) is derived from the "Shanghai Five" mechanism established by China, Russia, Kazakhstan, Kyrgyzstan and Tajikistan. On June 14, 2001 the top leaders of the "Shanghai Five" held their sixth summit in Shanghai, and Uzbekistan joined the group with full equality. On the following day, the six members signed the declaration on the founding of the SCO. The heads of the SCO member states meet once a year, and their heads of government meet on a regular basis. The member states host their meetings by turns.

In June 2002 the heads of the SCO member states signed the SCO Charter. It is stipulated in the Charter that the main goals and tasks of the SCO are to strengthen mutual trust, friendship and good-neighborliness between the member states;

to consolidate multidisciplinary cooperation in the maintenance and strengthening of peace, security and stability in the region and the promotion of a new democratic, fair and rational political and economic international order; to jointly counteract terrorism, separatism and extremism in all their manifestations, to fight against illicit narcotics and arms trafficking and other types of criminal activity of a transnational character, as well as illegal migration; to encourage efficient regional cooperation in such spheres as politics, trade and economy, defense, law enforcement, environmental protection, culture, science and technology, education, energy, transport, credit and finance, and other spheres of common interest. In 2004 the SCO initiated an observer mechanism and granted observer status to Mongolia, Pakistan, Iran and India, successively, thereby expanding into the Middle East and Indian subcontinent. The SCO thus became the organization with the largest geographical scope in Eurasia.

中非合作论坛
Forum on China-Africa Cooperation

The Forum on China-Africa Cooperation (FOCAC), founded in 2000, is a mechanism for collective dialogue and cooperation to cope with challenges posed by the new international situation and economic globalization, and to facilitate common development. The Forum approved the Beijing Declaration of the FOCAC and the Program for China-Africa Cooperation in Economic and Social Development at the First Ministerial Conference in Beijing, capital of China, in October 2000, and the FOCAC Addis Ababa Action Plan (2004-2006) at the Second Ministerial Conference in Addis Ababa, capital of Ethiopia, in December 2003. The Chinese government worked out series of policies and measures for assisting the development of Africa and promoting Sino-African cooperation within the framework of the FOCAC. On January 12, 2006 the Chinese government issued a paper on China's African policy. Through this paper, the Chinese government presented to the world the objectives of China's policy toward Africa and the measures to achieve them, and its proposals for cooperation in various fields in the coming years, with a view to promoting the steady growth of long-term Sino-African relations and bringing the concerned countries' mutually-beneficial cooperation to a new stage.

The Summit of the Forum on China-Africa Cooperation was held in Beijing from November 4 to 6, 2006.

The Beijing Summit and the Third Ministerial Conference of the FOCAC were convened from November 3 to 5, 2006. The heads of state or government and delegates from 48 African countries and China attended the meeting and endorsed the Declaration of FOCAC Beijing Summit and the FOCAC Beijing Action Plan (2007-2009) for the purpose of fostering friendship, peace, cooperation and development. The two documents proclaimed the establishment of a new type of strategic partnership between China and Africa and mapped out China-Africa cooperation in all fields for the following three years. At the Beijing Summit, Chinese President Hu Jintao announced eight steps that the Chinese government would take to forge a new type of Sino-African strategic partnership:

1. Double its 2006 assistance to Africa by 2009;

2. Provide US$ three billion in preferential loans and US$ two billion in preferential buyer's credits to Africa in the following three years;

3. Set up a Sino-African development fund of up to US$ five billion to encourage Chinese companies to invest in Africa, and provide support for them;

4. Build a conference center for the African Union to support African countries in their efforts to strengthen themselves through unity and support the process of African integration;

5. Cancel debts in the form of all interest-free government loans which matured at the end of 2005, owed by the heavily indebted poor countries and the least developed countries in Africa that have diplomatic relations with China;

6. Further open up China's markets to Africa by increasing from 190 to over 440 the number of items imported tariff-free by China from the least developed countries in Africa having diplomatic ties with China;

7. Establish three to five trade and economic cooperation zones in Africa in the following three years;

8. Over the following three years, train 15,000 African professionals; send 100 senior agricultural experts to Africa; set up ten special agricultural technology demonstration centers in Africa; build 30 hospitals in Africa and provide RMB 300 million for supplying artemisinin and building 30 malaria prevention and treatment centers; dispatch 300 young volunteers; build 100

rural schools; and increase the number of Chinese government scholarships to African students from the current 2,000 per year to 4,000 per year by 2009.

博鳌亚洲论坛

Boao Forum for Asia

On February 27, 2001 delegates from 26 countries, including China, India, Indonesia, Japan and Uzbekistan, met in Boao, Hainan Province, China and proclaimed the founding of the Boao Forum for Asia (BFA). As a non-government, non-profit, regular international organization, the BFA set Boao as its permanent headquarters, and Chinese and English as its official languages. The Forum is a prestigious platform for leaders in government, business and academia in Asia and other continents to share their visions for the significant issues in this dynamic region and the world at large. The BFA is committed to promoting regional economic integration, and bringing Asian countries closer to their development goals.

The Forum was initiated in 1998 by Fidel Ramos, former President of the Philippines, Bob Hawke, former Prime Minister of Australia, and Morihiro Hosokawa, former Prime Minister of Japan. Countries across the region have responded with strong support, and the rest of the world has paid close attention. The BFA has held annual meetings in Hainan since 2002.

电子政务

E-government

The Chinese government has been reinforcing its e-government since entering the 21st century. The website of the Central People's Government of the People's Republic of China (www.gov.cn) was officially open to the public on January 1, 2006. The website is a platform for the State Council and the ministries and commissions under it, and the governments of the provinces, autonomous regions and municipalities directly under the central government to publish information about government affairs and provide online services.

Related data shows that China's e-government market reached RMB 47.8 billion in 2005, and 93.4 percent of ministries and commissions under the State Council have their own websites; among local governments at the provincial, district and county levels the percentages are 90.3, 93.1 and 69.3 percent, respectively. The main objectives of China's e-government during the 11th Five-Year Plan period (2006-2010) are to basically establish a unified e-government network nationwide and a mechanism for publicizing and sharing information resources, and to build the official websites of governments at all levels into key channels for publicizing government information, with more than 50 percent of administrative licensing items handled online. As a result, e-government will play a larger role in enhancing the public service and supervision capability of the government, and lowering administrative costs.

中国十大杰出青年

China's Top 10 Outstanding Young People

China's Top 10 Outstanding Young People Awards are sponsored by the All-China Youth Federation, China Youth Development Foundation and ten major media agencies of Beijing. The Awards are aimed at commending and publicizing excellent young people who have made outstanding contributions to socialist construction with Chinese characteristics and to building a positive image of modern Chinese young people. The Award has been conferred annually since 1990.

The steps for selecting the winners are as follows: First, Committees of the Communist Youth League (CYL) and Youth Federations at the provincial level submit local nominees; second, the organizing committee selects 30 candidates from the nominees; third, the candidates are publicized in the media for a month; finally the judging committee votes for the ten winners of the Awards. Thanks to the influence of this national Awards, almost all provinces, autonomous regions and municipalities directly under the central government have selected their own Top Ten Outstanding Young People. Different trades and industries have done the same as well. In addition, the CYL Central Committee and the China Volunteers Association jointly sponsor the Top 10 Outstanding Young Volunteers Awards, the highest prizes for young volunteers in China.

感动中国

Touching China

Touching China: Person of the Year is an annual TV program made by China Central Television (CCTV), China's national TV station, since 2002. At the end of each year, the significant events of the year are reviewed by focusing on the touching stories about ten persons and one group selected nationwide. Touching China has become the most influential and authoritative among all the media activities for selecting the Person of the Year in China. The organizing committee of the program seeks candidates nationwide, and counts the votes and the suggestions of audiences, readers and netizens, and then announces the results at the CCTV awards ceremony. All the candidates, whether well-known or not, are people whose lives and work touch people's hearts.

Besides Touching China, CCTV also carries programs selecting the country's Economic Person of the Year and Judge of the Year.

新闻发言人

Public Information Officer

This refers to a news release system for promoting the openness and transparency of government affairs, and strengthening contacts between organs of administration and the people. In a sense, the public information officer is an "authorized mouthpiece." As early as in the 1950s, China started releasing news in this way. For instance, Chen Yi, the then Vice-premier of the State Council and Minister of Foreign Affairs held a press conference on May 29, 1962; the Central Foreign Publicity Leadership Group drafted the Proposal for Establishing the Public Information Officer System in early 1982; in February 1983 the Central Publicity Department and the Central Foreign Publicity Leadership Group jointly issued the Opinions on the Implementation of the Public Information Officer System and Improving the Work Concerning Foreign Journalists, which required the Foreign Ministry and ministries and commissions under the State Council with foreign contacts to set up a news release system.

China's first Public Information Officer was appointed in 1983 in recognition of the need for foreign publicity, when Qian Qichen, the then Director of the Information Department of the Ministry of Foreign Affairs appeared as a speaker at the press conferences of the Ministry of Foreign Affairs. As a result, the Ministry of Foreign Affairs became the first ministry of China to set up a Public Information Officer system, and has demonstrated the best implementation of the system. In September 2003 the Information Office of the State Council launched a training program for Public Information Officers nationwide.

三个意识

Three Awarenesses

When attending the Chongqing delegation's discussion on the government work report during the Fifth Session of the 10th National People's Congress on March 8, 2007, Chinese President Hu Jintao exhorted the cadres at all levels, especially those in leadership positions, to "enhance their awareness of adversity and always maintain a pioneering and enterprising spirit; enhance their awareness of public service and always keep the principle of serving the people wholeheartedly in mind; enhance their awareness of frugality, carry forward the spirit of struggle against all hardships, and unite and lead the broad masses of the people to obtain successes in the reform and opening-up, and socialist modernization drive."

China faces both challenges and opportunities in this period of strategic choices for accelerating reform and opening-up, and development. President Hu Jintao called upon cadres in leadership positions to grasp the opportunities and tackle the challenges by highlighting the "Three Awarenesses." Only with enhanced awareness of adversity can leadership cadres at all levels intensify their sense of responsibility and mission toward the country and the people, maintain a pioneering and enterprising spirit, handle all kinds of challenges and difficulties, and work hard. Only with enhanced awareness of public service can cadres overcome bureaucratism and formalism, serve the people more sincerely, and lead them to build a harmonious society. Only with elevated awareness of frugality can cadres retain the spirit of struggle against all hardships, oppose waste, cope with the shortage of resources and low environmental quality, and guide the people to build an energy-efficient society and a modernized country.

经济

Economy

可持续发展

Sustainable Development

This is a new concept put forth in the 1980s. In 1987, the World Commission on Environment and Development defined in *Our Common Future* the concept of sustainable development, which was widely acknowledged all over the world. Sustainable development was defined as: "Meeting the needs of the present without compromising the ability of future generations to meet their own needs." To be specific, the coordinated development of the economy, society, resources and environmental protection should achieve the goal of developing the economy while also protecting natural resources and the environment, including the atmosphere, water, oceans, land and forests that mankind depends on, enabling future generations to live and develop continuously in a good environment.

During the Tenth Five-Year Plan period (2001-2005), the average annual growth of China's GDP was around 9.5 percent. In 2005, this figure reached 18,232.1 billion yuan (about US$ 2,225.7 billion), and the per capita GDP was US$ 1,700. Total imports and exports increased from US$ 474.3 billion-worth in 2000 to US$ 1,421.9 billion-worth in 2005, ranking third in the world. China's foreign exchange reserve in 2005 reached US$ 818.9 billion, ranking second in the world. However, China had not yet done enough for its sustainable development. The "four major indices"—the amount of cultivated land reserved, pollutant discharge amount, proportion of input into R&D to GDP, and enrollment rate of senior high schools—did not meet the goals set in the Tenth Five-Year Plan. In 2005, the discharge amount of industrial solid waste dropped remarkably, but the goal of reducing other major pollutants (such as sulfur dioxide and soot) by 10 percent was not achieved, and the discharge amount of sulfur dioxide even increased. It is an important task during the 11th Five-Year Plan period (2006-2010) to change the extensive economic growth mode and promote coordinated development.

小康社会
Well-off Society

This concept was put forth by Deng Xiaoping, the architect of China's reform and opening-up in connection with the goal of achieving modernization at the end of the 20th century. He said, "The first step in our goal is to set up a well-off society by 2000." The 12th National Congress of the Communist Party of China (CPC) formally quoted this concept, and made it a strategic goal for the end of the 20th century. In a well-off society, the quality of the people's life is further improved on the basis of adequate food and clothing. The overall targets to build a well-off society in an all-round way are: to quadruple the 2000 GDP by 2020; basically achieve industrialization; rank among the top three countries in the world in terms of comprehensive national power; and basically meet the requirements for sustainable development and a benign cycle.

The basic criteria for building a well-off society in an all-round way cover ten aspects: 1) the per capita GNP should exceed US$ 3,000, which is the fundamental symbol of a well-off society; 2) the annual per capita disposable income of urban residents should reach 18,000 yuan; 3) the annual per capita net income of rural residents should rise to 8,000 yuan; 4) the Engel coefficient should be lower than 40 percent; 5) the per capita living space for urban residents should be 30 sq m; 6) the urbanization rate should reach 50 percent; 7) the computer popularization rate in Chinese households should reach 20 percent; 8) the college enrollment rate should reach 20 percent; 9) there should be 2.8 doctors per 1,000 people; and 10) the guarantee of subsistence allowances for urban residents should cover 95 percent of the urban population living below poverty line.

“三步走”战略

The Three-step Development Strategy

The Chinese government has a clear and definite objective for economic development, known as the Three-step Development Strategy, set out in 1987.

Step One—to double the 1980 GNP and ensure that the people have enough food and clothing—was attained by the end of the 1980s. Step Two—to quadruple the 1980 GNP by the end of the 20th century—was achieved in 1995, ahead of schedule. Step Three—to increase the per capita GNP to the level of the medium-developed countries by the mid-21st century—at which point, the Chinese people will be fairly well-off and modernization will be basically realized.

两个“一百”

Two “Centenaries”

The two “centenaries” are long-term plans for the economic and social development of China. They were proposed by the 13th Central Committee of the Communist Party of China (CPC) in the report to the 14th National Congress of the CPC in October 1992.

The report pointed out that China would set up a new economic system by the 1990s, achieving the second step of the Three-step Development Strategy; by 2021, the centenary of the CPC, China would have a mature and fixed system regarding every aspect; and on this basis, by 2049, the centenary of the founding of the People's Republic of China, China would achieve the third step of the Three-step Development Strategy, basically realizing socialist modernization.

五个统筹
"Five Balances"

On October 14, 2003, the Third Plenary Session of the 16th Central Committee of the CPC approved the Decision of the Central Committee of the Communist Party of China on Some Issues Concerning the Improvement of the Socialist Market Economy, proposing that while building a well-off society in an all-round way, China should implement the "Five Balances"—balancing urban and rural development, balancing development among regions, balancing economic and social development, balancing the development of man and Nature, and balancing domestic development with opening wider to the outside world.

It is a new concept of development. China's agriculture is underdeveloped, and farmers' incomes are increasing slowly, an important factor hindering economic growth. The key to building a well-off society in an all-round way lies in the farmers. To solve problems concerning "agriculture, the countryside and the farmers" the Chinese government has to pay more attention to the balanced development of urban and rural areas and urban-rural integration, instead of simply supporting and improving agriculture. To balance development among regions demands that the central government continue pushing forward the plan for the development of the western regions, give full play to the comprehensive advantages of central China, make efforts to rejuvenate the old industrial bases in Northeast China and encourage eastern areas with mature conditions to pilot the basic stages of modernization. To balance economic and social development means that the development of social undertakings cannot be allowed to always lag behind economic development, and importance should be attached to public management, social security, health care, education, culture, etc. To balance the development of man and Nature embodies the modern ideas of environmental protection, ecological protection and putting people first, and is an important achievement of man's reflection on his activities, which also benefits posterity. The demand to balance domestic development and opening wider to the outside world is the summary of China's experience and lessons learned over 100 years, and the acknowledgement of China's being in line with international practice.

经济普查
Economic Census

As approved by the State Council, the economic census of China is an integrated one covering secondary and tertiary industries, and basic units, as well as construction. The first national economic census started on December 31, 2004. It will be conducted twice every ten years, in those years with the numbers ending "3" and "8". The economic census targets enterprises, institutions, state organs, social organizations, and self-employed individuals, and aims to ascertain the development of the secondary and tertiary industries.

The Economic Census of China is designed to help keep abreast of the development of the secondary and tertiary industries in our country in terms of their scales, structures and economic achievements, and establish a sound system of registers and databases of the basic units, providing a foundation for conducting studies to make plans for national socio-economic development and raising the level of policy-making and management. Data were collected from eight million impersonal entities and industrial units, and nearly 30 million self-employed individuals engaged in the secondary and tertiary industries within the territory of the People's Republic of China. The census employed about ten million enumerators and assistants.

资源节约型社会

Energy-Efficient Society

In October 2005, the Fifth Plenary Session of the 16th Central Committee of the CPC formally approved the building of an energy-efficient and environmentally-friendly society as a strategic task of the middle- and long-term plan for economic and social development. An energy-efficient society takes legal, economic and administrative measures in the fields of production, distribution and consumption to increase the efficiency of energy utilization, and thus reaps the maximum economic and social returns with the least resources consumed, and guarantees the sustainable social and economic development.

The economic development of China is facing three challenges: deficient resources, wasted energy and deteriorating environment. Although China's gross reserves of resources rank third in the world, the large population means the per capita quantity of resources rank 53rd, only half of the world's average per capita quantity. Thus, China is a country short of resources. The phenomenon of waste of resources exists from production to consumption, as the Chinese people have a weak sense of resource saving and recycling. The economic development of China has severely damaged the natural environment, and consequently an environmental crisis looms, and incidents of air pollution, grassland degeneration, rivers running dry and industrial pollution occur frequently. According to the Environmental Sustainability Index released by the 2005 World Economic Forum held in Davos, Switzerland, China ranks 133rd among the 144 countries and regions around the world. To build an energy-efficient society is an important amendment to the previous approach to the economic development of China over the past two decades, and also a good way to improve public ethics.

循环经济
Recycling Economy

A recycling economy centers on the highly efficient use and recycling of resources, follows the principles of reduced use, reusing and recycling, and features low consumption, low discharge and high efficiency. It is a kind of growth pattern conforming to the idea of sustainable development, a complete revolution compared to the traditional growth pattern featuring "mass production, mass consumption and mass waste." Over the past more than 20 years, China has paid a high price for its rapid and sustained economic growth. According to the Chinese Academy of Sciences, in 2003 China accounted for 31 percent of the world's raw coal consumption, 30 percent of its iron ore consumption, 27 percent of its steel consumption and 40 percent of its cement consumption. At the same time, its GDP accounted for less than four percent of the world's total. This wasteful growth pattern resulted in shortages of coal, electricity, oil and transportation. Although the Chinese government has strengthened its macro-control, the bottleneck problem of resources is still urgent. China's 2004 Central Economic Work Conference proposed promoting the recycling economy.

The key work for developing the recycling economy includes: saving energy, water, land and materials; promoting in an all-round way clean production to reduce waste from the source, and realizing the transformation from end treatment to pollution prevention and control of the whole production process; making comprehensive use of resources, and recycling waste and renewable resources to the maximum extent; and developing the environmental protection industry so as to provide technical support for the efficient use of resources, recycling and reducing waste discharge.

绿色 GDP

Green GDP

Green GDP (green gross domestic product) is the adjusted GDP minus environmental costs input into economic activities.

Green GDP accounting refers to an accounting system deducting natural resources depletion costs and environmental degradation costs, so as to assess the quality of economic development in the real sense. The Green GDP Accounting Research Project was jointly launched by the State Environmental Protection Administration (SEPA) and the National Bureau of Statistics (NBS) in March 2004. In September 2006, the *China Green GDP Accounting Report 2004* was released, the first report to appear in China on environmentally-adjusted GDP accounting. The report shows that the input treatment cost of environmental pollution accounted for 1.8 percent of the GDP. In 2004, economic losses caused by environmental pollution reached 511.8 billion yuan-worth, accounting for 3.05 percent of the GDP in 2004. Of this figure, the cost due to water pollution came to 286.28 billion yuan, accounting for 55.9 percent of the total; the cost due to air pollution, 219.80 billion yuan, accounting for 42.9 percent; and the cost due to solid wastes and pollution accidents, 5.74 billion yuan, accounting for 1.2 percent. An integrated environmental and economic accounting system should cover at least five types of natural resources depletion costs (land, minerals, forest, water and fishery resources) and two types of environmental degradation costs (environmental pollution cost and ecological damage cost). The 2004 accounting report only represented the environmental pollution costs, which should have included the costs of over 20 items. But because of the limitations of basic data and techniques, the accounting results in 2004 only covered the costs of ten items. Groundwater, soil contamination and other key items were not discussed.

"十一五"规划
The 11th Five-Year Plan

China's five-year plans aim to set major targets for national economic and social development during each plan period; arrange the distribution of the productive forces and individual sector contributions to the national economy, and set the targeted economic growth rate and output of industrial and agricultural products; estimate the growth of living standards; map the scale and direction of investment in fixed assets and arrange national key construction projects; put forward major targets for social undertakings; decide on important economic and technological policies; and make specific measures for the implementation of the plan. Since the founding of the People's Republic of China in 1949, except for a period of economic recovery from October 1949 to December 1952 and a period of economic adjustment from 1963 to 1965, China has drawn up and implemented ten five-year plans between 1953 and 2005. In 2006 China started to implement the 11th Five-Year Plan for National Economic and Social Development (2006-2010).

The 11th Five-Year Plan set the following major goals for national economic development: 1) Stable development of the national economy while maintaining an annual GDP growth of 7.5 percent and doubling the per capita GDP for the year 2000; an addition of 90 million new jobs, half of which for urban residents and the rest for migrant workers from the countryside; maintenance of stable prices and international revenue and expenditure. 2) Optimizing and upgrading the industrial structure, including making the industrial, product and enterprise structures more rational; raising the added value of tertiary industry in the GDP by three percentage points; raising tertiary industry employment by four percentage points in the total labor force; enhancing independent innovation capability and increasing the proportion of the expenditure on scientific research and experiments to two percent of the GDP; and developing enterprises with independent intellectual property rights and famous brands, and strong international competitiveness. 3) A marked growth in the efficient utilization of resources, with energy consumption per-unit GDP decreasing by 20 percent, water consumption per-unit industrial added value decreasing by 30 percent, utilization coefficient for agricultural irrigation water growing to 0.5, and the comprehensive ratio for solid industrial residue used increasing to 60 percent. 4) Enhancing the capability for sustainable development by maintaining 120 million ha of cultivated land and intensifying the protection of fresh water, energy and important mineral resources, putting under control the deteriorating trend of the ecological environment, reducing the total volume of released major pollutants by 10 percent, increasing the forest coverage to 20 percent and controlling greenhouse gas emission. 5) Perfecting the market economic system by making breakthroughs in the reform and mechanism setup of the administration, State-owned enterprises, finance and taxation, and banking, greatly enhancing the capability of market supervision and social management, coordinating the opening-up and domestic development in a better way and promoting the opening of the economy to a new level. 6) Continually improving the people's life, with an annual increase of five percent for the per capita disposable income of urban residents and for the per capita net income of rural residents, overall improvement in the quality of life of both urban and rural residents, and remarkable improvement of the conditions of housing, communication, culture and environment.

西部大开发

Development of Western China

In 2000, China started the Western Development campaign. The western region includes six provinces—Sichuan, Guizhou, Yunnan, Shaanxi, Gansu and Qinghai—five autonomous regions —Tibet, Ningxia, Xinjiang, Inner Mongolia and Guangxi—and one municipality—Chongqing. This region covers an area of 6,850,000 sq km, accounting for 71.4 percent of the national territory; and it has a total population of 372 million (by the end of 2004), accounting for 28.6 percent of the national total. Western China is rich in minerals (nonferrous metal, rare earth, etc.), energy (including hydropower, coal, oil and natural gas), tourism and land resources, and is thus considered the second "golden" area for opening up. Western China has six advantageous industries: energy and chemicals, mineral exploitation and processing, agricultural product and livestock processing, equipment manufacturing, hi-tech industry and tourism.

From 2000 to 2005, western China witnessed an average annual growth of 10.6 percent in total output value, and 15.7 percent in local fiscal revenue. Altogether, 70 important construction projects were started there, involving some 1,000 billion yuan. In early March 2007, the National Development and Reform Commission issued the 11th Five-Year Plan for Western Region Development, putting forward the goals of "one stable" and "three new." "One stable" means putting the starting point for achieving healthy and rapid economic development on the sustained and stable improvement of the people's livelihood, with emphasis on the principle of putting people first. On the basis of increasing the quality of and returns from economic development, the region will work to double the per capita regional output value in 2000 by the end of 2010. The trend of increasing disparity between per capita income in western China and the national average will be curtailed, and an annual increase of six percent for the per capita disposable income of urban residents and for the per capita net income of rural residents will be achieved. In addition, impoverished people will have enough food and clothing, and low-income people will see their income increase on a stable basis. "Three new" refers to new breakthroughs in infrastructure construction and environmental improvement, new levels of development in key areas and major industries, and new achievements in equalizing basic public services.

振兴东北

Rejuvenation of Northeast China

In 2002, the 16th CPC National Congress proposed to rejuvenate the old industrial bases in Northeast China. This area consists of Liaoning, Jilin and Heilongjiang provinces, covering a total area of over 800,000 sq km and having a total population of over 100 million. Since China adopted the policy of reform and opening-up in 1978, Northeast China has been developing more slowly than the coastal areas of East China due to the heavy burdens of State-owned enterprises and other reasons, and the total industrial output value of the three provinces only accounts for 60 percent of that of Guangdong. But Northeast China has a good industrial foundation, rich natural resources and a contingent of skilled technicians. The key to its rejuvenation lies in institutional innovation. The strategic decision to rejuvenate Northeast China can help to achieve balanced development among China's regions.

Rural taxation reform, restructuring of State-owned enterprises, transformation of resource-based cities, and reform of the social security system are important parts of the program to rejuvenate Northeast China. In the past few years, since the strategy of rejuvenating Northeast China was introduced, the economic development of those old industrial bases has been speeded up. In 2005, the total output value of Liaoning grew by 12.3 percent, that of Jilin, by 12 percent, and that of Heilongjiang, by 11.6 percent; the total output of grain in these three provinces reached a record 79.3 million tons; the per capita disposable income of urban residents in Liaoning, Jilin and Heilongjiang grew by 12.8 percent, 10.8 percent and 10.7 percent, respectively, higher than the national average growth rate

(9.6 percent); the per capita net income of rural residents grew by 7.3 percent, 8.8 percent and 7.2 percent respectively, higher than the national average growth rate (6.2 percent). From January to June 2006, the GDP of the three provinces reached 779.91 billion yuan, an increase of 12.2 percent compared to that of the same period of the previous year and 1.2 percentage points higher than the national average.

中部崛起

Rise of Central China

In the 1980s, the Development Research Center of the State Council proposed to prevent the "sinking (lagging) of central China." Central China lags greatly behind the national overall or average level, especially that of the coastal areas in East China, in the aspects of economic aggregate, development level and speed, industrialization, urbanization and marketization, and structural changes. In 2004, the State Council put forth a proposal to "promote the rise of Central China" in the government work report to the National People's Congress. Central China includes Hunan, Hubei, Henan, Shanxi, Anhui and Jiangxi provinces, with a total area of over 10 percent of the national territory and nearly 30 percent of the total population of China.

The policy for promoting the rise of Central China can be summarized as "two extends" and "two supports." "Two extends" refers to, first, extending the policies for rejuvenating the old industrial bases in Northeast China to key industrial cities and resource-based cities in central China, such as VAT transformation and the reform of State-owned enterprises; second, extending the policies supporting the development of western China to central China, for example, extending the policies for western countryside development, urban development and the eco-environment building to mountainous areas, old revolutionary base areas and impoverished areas in central China. "Two supports" refers to, first, supporting for the development of the grain industry, because central China is a major grain-producing area and a key support point for national grain security; second, the special support the government gives to central China in developing competitive industries (including energy and raw materials), transportation and modern logistics, building up the circulation system, building a new countryside, and developing groups of cities.

长三角

Yangtze River Delta

The Yangtze River Delta is a low, flat, triangular stretch of alluvial land at the estuary of the Yangtze River. In economic terms, it refers to the industrial and economic belt covering central and southern Jiangsu province and northeastern Zhejiang province, with Shanghai playing the leading role. It is an economic zone with the fastest development speed, largest economic aggregate and most potential in China. It contains 16 cities—Shanghai Municipality; Nanjing, Suzhou, Yangzhou, Zhenjiang, Taizhou, Wuxi, Changzhou and Nantong in Jiangsu Province; and Hangzhou, Ningbo, Huzhou, Jiaxing, Zhoushan, Shaoxing and Taizhou in Zhejiang Province.

The Development Report on China's Regional Economy 2006, published by the Chinese Academy of Social Sciences, points out that the Yangtze River Delta will remain the most developed zone in China. However, in 2005, although the Delta maintained stable economic growth, its growth rate slowed down. In the first three quarters of 2005, the GDP growth rate of the Delta fell 2.6 percentage points, while the national GDP growth rate only decreased 0.1 percent. Therefore, the Yangtze River Delta should change from its previous "extensive growth mode" to an "intensive growth mode" which has high technology content, low resource consumption and low environmental pollution, and is able to generate good economic results and give full play to human resources.

A view of Pudong, Shanghai

珠三角

Zhujiang (Pearl) River Delta

In 1994, Guangdong Province made a plan for interregional economic development, and brought forth, for the first time,

Shenzhen, a thriving metropolis, used to be a fishing village only two decades ago.

the concept of the Zhujiang River Delta Economic Zone, which covers seven cities—Guangzhou, Shenzhen, Zhuhai, Dongguan, Foshan, Zhongshan and Jiangmen—and parts of three cities—Huizhou, Qingyuan and Zhaoqing. The population of the Delta accounts for six percent of the national total, but its export amount takes up one third of the national total. The Delta is one of the four industrial bases of China, and one of the three "economic circles" (the others are the Yangtze River Delta and the Beijing-Tianjin-Hebei Economic Circle); it and the Yangtze River Delta are called "the two big engines propelling China's economy."

The Development Report on China's Regional Economy 2006, published by the Chinese Academy of Social Sciences, points out that the Zhujiang River Delta is still the most active economic development zone in China. By the end of 2004, the per capita

GDP of the Zhujiang River Delta had exceeded US$5,200, approaching the standard of moderately developed countries. At present, in the hinterland of the Zhujiang River Delta which used to be dominated by light industries, capital- and technology-concentrated areas and projects are changing the pattern of the Delta, such as the Dayawan Petrochemical Town managed by the CNOOC and Shell Petrochemicals Co., Ltd., Guangzhou Automobile Town with factories run by Toyota, Nissan and Honda of Japan, and the Nansha Heavy Chemical Industrial Zone, with steel and shipbuilding playing the leading role. The Zhujiang River Delta High- and New-Technology Belt has always been a locomotive of high- and new-technology. In 2005, its new- and hi-tech products had an output value of over 580 billion yuan.

泛长三角

Pan-Yangtze River Delta

The "3+2" mode is considered the most realistic way to build a Pan-Yangtze River Delta Economic Zone beyond the geographical range of the Delta. Many scholars believe that the economic integration in the Yangtze River Delta should not be restricted in the scope of "15+1" cities, and thus proposed the concept of the "3+2" mode. The new mode includes Jiangsu, Zhejiang and Shanghai as well as Anhui and Jiangxi provinces on the middle and lower reaches of the Yangtze River; together they are called the Pan-Yangtze River Delta Economic Zone.

Many experts and scholars believe that the building of the Pan-Yangtze River Delta has at least two advantages compared with the Pan-Zhujiang River Delta.

First is convenient transportation. There are no less than 20 main lines of communication, including expressways, railways, high-speed rail and national highways linking Anhui and Jiangxi with Jiangsu, Zhejiang and Shanghai and forming a regional transportation network. Moreover, the Yangtze River is a "golden watercourse" with a transportation capacity equal to that of several railways. Moreover, looking a little bit further to the west one finds that the Yangtze River links the Delta with Hunan and Hubei provinces. Therefore the transportation conditions of the Pan-Yangtze River Delta are far better that those of the Pan-Zhujiang River Delta.

Second is the advantage of similar geo-cultures. Just as Zhejiang and southern Jiangsu, southern Anhui and Jiangxi are also in the areas south of the lower reaches of the Yangtze River, and thus have similar geo-cultures. Northern Anhui and northern Jiangsu are in the central area of the Huihe River basin and also have similar geo-cultures. As the geo-cultures of the Pan-Yangtze River Delta are closer than those of the Pan-Zhujiang River Delta, they play a more important role in regional economic development.

泛珠三角
Pan-Zhujiang River Delta

In July 2003, Guangdong Province came up with the idea of a Pan-Zhujiang River Delta, which covers Fujian, Jiangxi, Guangxi, Hainan, Hunan, Sichuan, Yunnan, Guizhou and Guangdong, neighbors in the Zhujiang River basin with close economic cooperation between them, plus the Hong Kong and Macao special administrative regions. The idea is called "9+2" for short. The nine provinces and autonomous region (Guangxi) have a total area accounting for one fifth of the national territory, a total population making up one third of the national total, and economic aggregate occupying one third of the national total. In June 2004 regional cooperation in the Pan-Zhujiang River Delta was formally launched.

From 2003 to the end of July 2006, departments and organizations in the Pan-Zhujiang River Delta signed 65 agreements altogether. On the whole, the growth rate of the gross regional product (GRP) in this region has risen remarkably since 2003, reaching 10 percent or above; only Hong Kong's economy slipped because of the SARS epidemic. In 2004, except for Hong Kong, this whole region witnessed a GRP growth rate of over 14 percent, and Macao's GRP grew by 30 percent. At present, the Pan-Zhujiang River Delta has two big opportunities: Guangdong's industries are experiencing structural transformation, and the western Zhujiang River Delta needs to be further developed. In recent years, Guangdong has been actively promoting heavy industry, including automobiles and petrochemical, while related industries can provide raw materials for downstream Hong Kong enterprises to help them save costs and improve their export competitiveness. Moreover, the service industry of Hong Kong can also find great potential for trade and benefits in Guangdong's development.

多种经济成分并存

Diverse Forms of Ownership Existing Side by Side

Before 1978, China only had public ownership, with state-owned enterprises making up 77.6 percent and collectively-owned enterprises making up 22.4 percent. The reform and opening up policies created a large space for the development of diverse forms of ownership in the economy. Foreign, Hong Kong, Macao and Taiwan-invested enterprises, and individual and privately-run enterprises mushroomed.

The reform of state-owned enterprises has always been the core of China's economic reform. The Chinese government has tried every means to solve the problem of long-term losses for state-owned enterprises. At present, China has almost finished reforming state-owned enterprises into joint-stock corporations, and they have witnessed a sustained rally of economic returns and a marked increase of overall strength and quality. In fact, they have become the mainstay of China's economy. By 2005, of the added value created by all industrial enterprises with annual sales of over five million yuan each, state-owned enterprises and enterprises whose controlling stake was owned by the State accounted for 39.2 percent, collectively-owned enterprises took up 3.9 percent, and non-public-owned enterprises (foreign, Hong Kong, Macao and Taiwan-invested enterprises, and individual and privately-run enterprises) accounted for the rest. This showed a dynamic situation of the coexistence of diverse forms of ownership in the economy.

中国制造

Made in China

"Made in China" is a general name for all the products produced in China. It appeared in China in the 1970s, and now has gone overseas and can be found everywhere around the world. At present, most Chinese brands are practical but inexpensive. Although "Made in China" can be found in many countries and enjoys a good reputation, most products with the "Made in China" label are small and cheap articles.

One reason for China's becoming a large manufacturing country is the low price of its products. But the major factor contributing to the low price is cheap labor power, and not technological innovation. Former Minister of Commerce Bo Xilai once said, "China buys one Airbus 380 at the cost of selling 800 million shirts." This highlighted the dilemma of "Made in China": China produces low-end products, from which it makes meager profits, and thus stays in a disadvantageous position in the global value chain. The only solution to "Made in China" is to change the structure of the country's export products, and this can only be done by ensuring intellectual property rights and increasing the technology content of products by technological innovation.

利用外资

Utilizing Foreign Investment

China has diverse channels and forms for utilizing foreign investment, which can be roughly divided into three kinds: borrowing from foreign countries, including loans offered by foreign governments, international banking organizations and foreign commercial banks, export credits, and issuing bonds in foreign countries; foreign direct investment (FDI) in the forms of Sino-foreign joint ventures, cooperative businesses, wholly foreign-owned enterprises, and cooperative projects; and other foreign investments, such as international leasing, compensation trade, assembly and stock issued in foreign countries. From 1979 to 2005, the foreign investment in actual use in China totaled US$ 809.2 billion, of which FDI accounted for US$ 622.4 billion.

Since the early 1980s, China has input manpower, and physical and financial resources to build infrastructure in many places, creating a good environment for foreign investment. Meanwhile, the National People's Congress and the State Council have issued over 500 foreign-related economic laws and regulations, providing a legal foundation and guarantee for foreign investment in China. At the end of 1997, China revised and released the Catalogue of Industries for Guiding Foreign Investment, encouraging and supporting foreign investors in the fields of comprehensive development of agriculture, energy, transportation, major raw materials, high- and new-technology, comprehensive utilization of resources, and environmental protection. According to the WTO rules and China's commitments, China has basically completed revising its foreign-related economic laws and regulations, and set up a legal framework with the Law on Chinese-Foreign Equity Joint Ventures, Law on Chinese-Foreign Contractual Joint Ventures and Law on Foreign Capital Enterprises, and the regulations for the implementation of these three basic laws. By the end of 2005, China had received foreign investors from 192 countries and regions, and the number of foreign-invested enterprises had reached 553,000. International financial groups and multinational corporations hold a positive attitude toward the Chinese market, and 450 companies of the world's top 500 have invested in China. China is appraised by world investors and financial circles as one of the countries with the best investment environment.

三峡工程

The Three Gorges Project

The Key Water Control Project at the Three Gorges on the Yangtze River, also called the Three Gorges Project for short, is the largest project of its kind in China, and even in the world. It is a critical project for controlling and developing the Yangtze River, and for generating economic results in flood prevention, electricity generation and shipping. In April 1992, at the Fifth Session of the Seventh National People's Congress, the delegates discussed and approved "the proposal to start the Three Gorges Project on the Yangtze River." In December 1994, the project was formally started on the basis of preliminary preparations. The project is in three phases spanning 17 years from 1993 to 2009.

Flood prevention is the starting point of the project. The Three Gorges Dam has a normal water level of 175 m, and a reservoir capacity of 22.15 billion cu m. The Three Gorges Hydropower Station has an installed gross capacity of 18.20 million kw, generating an annual average of 84.7 billion kw/h electricity. It is expected to become the biggest hydropower station in the world. After the Three Gorges Hydropower Station is put into operation, it will connect the Central China, East China and South China power grids into a giant trans-regional power grid, and can be connected with the North China, Northwest China, and Southwest China grids to form a national power system. Compared with coal-burning electricity generation the Three Gorges Hydropower Station will also generate enormous environmental benefits, as it will reduce the discharge of carbon dioxide by a big margin, sulfur dioxide by one to two million tons, carbon monoxide by 10,000 tons, oxynitride by 370,000 tons, and dust and waste residue to a large extent, thus alleviating environmental pollution and acid rain caused by the discharge of poisonous gases. Standing 38 km upstream of the Nanjin Pass, the Three Gorges Dam will be able to improve the navigation conditions from Chongqing to Hankou and thus satisfy the need for the long-term development of navigation on the upper and middle reaches of the Yangtze River.

西气东输

West-to-East Natural Gas Transmission Project

The West-to-East Natural Gas Transmission Project is a benchmark for the Chinese government's strategy of developing western China. It runs from Lunnan in the Tarim Basin in Xinjiang Uygur Autonomous Region in the west to Baihe Town, Shanghai in the east. Its major task is to transmit natural gas from the Tarim Basin to Henan, Anhui, Jiangsu, Zhejiang and Shanghai, and the pipeline runs through Xinjiang, Gansu, Ningxia, Shaanxi, Shanxi, Henan, Anhui, Jiangsu, Shanghai and Zhejiang. The project was started in July 2002; the whole line was completed and linked up in October 2004; and the project started the commercial supply of gas in December 2004. The main pipeline is about 4,000 km long, and had an annual capacity of transmitting 12 billion cu m of natural gas by 2007.

The West-to-East Natural Gas Transmission Project will continuously increase the proportion of natural gas among the various kinds of energy consumed by China, and thus change the structure of energy consumption. In early 2005, construction started on the China-Kazakhstan crude oil pipeline and the crude oil and petroleum pipelines in western China. Together with the completed West-to-East natural gas transmission pipeline, a huge energy "corridor" for transmitting oil and natural gas will be opened up.

南水北调

South-to-North Water Diversion Project

In October 1952, Mao Zedong said, "South China has

abundant water resources, while North China has few. If possible, we can borrow water from the south." His proposal initiated the South-to-North Water Diversion Project. After dozens of years of study, planning got under way in June 2000 to divert water from the upper, middle and lower reaches of the Yangtze River to satisfy the development needs of Northwest and North China. Water from South China will be diverted to the north via three channels: west, central and east. These three and the Yangtze, Yellow, Huaihe and Haihe rivers will make up the major part of China's water-diversion network. By 2050, the total volume of water to be diverted through the three channels will reach 44.8 billion cu m. The whole project will be completed in stages.

Construction of the South-to-North Water Diversion Project started at the end of 2002. By the end of 2005, a total of 17 sub-projects had been completed, involving 57.35 million cu m of earth and stone, 68 percent of the total project under construction. During the 11th Five-Year Plan period (2006-2010), China will complete the Phase One projects for both the east and central channels as planned, so as to alleviate the water shortage in North China. At the same time, there will be a reasonable distribution of water sources from the Yangtze, Yellow, Huai and Hai rivers.

西电东送

West-to-East Electricity Transmission Project

The West-to-East Electricity Transmission Project is aimed at exploiting electricity resources in the western parts of the country, including Guizhou, Yunnan, Guangxi, Sichuan, Inner

Mongolia and Shaanxi, and transmitting them to Guangdong, Shanghai, Jiangsu, Zhejiang, Beijing, Tianjin and Tangshan, which are short of electricity. Hydro energy is unevenly distributed in China, with 90 percent of the exploitable installed capacity concentrated in the southwestern, south-central and northwestern regions. In particular, the mainstream and tributaries on the upper and middle reaches of the Yangtze River and many rivers in the southwestern region have an exploitable installed capacity accounting for 60 percent of the national total. Coal resources are also concentrated in Northwest and North China. However, the coastal areas in East China, where the economy is well developed, are short of energy, while seven provinces and municipalities in East China—Beijing, Tianjin, Shanghai, Jiangsu, Zhejiang, Shandong and Guangdong—consume over 40 percent of the national total of electricity.

On November 8, 2000, the construction of hydropower stations on the Wujiang River in western China's Guizhou Province was launched, marking the prelude to the West-to-East Electricity Transmission Project. The project features three lines –the southern one, which will transmit to Guangdong hydropower resources from the Wujiang River in Guizhou, Lancang River in Yunnan, as well as Nanpan, Beipan and Hongshui rivers at the borders of Guangxi, Yunnan and Guizhou, and electricity generated by power plants built near the mouths of coalmines in Guizhou and Yunnan; second is the central line transmitting to East China hydropower from the Yangtze River at the Three Gorges and the mainstream and tributaries of the Jinsha River; third is the northern line transmitting to Beijing, Tianjin and Tangshan hydropower from the upper reaches of the Yellow River and thermal power generated by power plants built near the mouths of coalmines in Inner Mongolia.

西煤东运
West-to-East Coal Transportation Project

This project aims to ship coal from western China to coastal areas in the east. In China, 64 percent of the coal resources are located in Shanxi, Shaanxi and western Inner Mongolia. Coal from these three places is transported eastward by railway, mostly on the northern, central and southern lines.

The major line for transporting coal from West China is the northern one, which consists of three railways: the Daqin Railway (from Datong in Shanxi to Qinhuangdao in Hebei), with a total length of over 600 km, whose transport capacity in 2005 reached 200 million tons, accounting for 65 percent of the total capacity of the northern line; second is the Shuohuang Railway (from Shenchi in Shanxi to Huanghua in Hebei) put into operation in 2002 and with a total length of 588 km, whose transport capacity in 2005 reached 68 million tons; third is a to-be-constructed double-track, heavy-load railway from Baotou and Jining in Inner Mongolia to Caofeidian and Jingtang Port in Hebei, with a total length of 740 km. The central line includes the Shijiazhuang-Taiyuan and Handan-Changzhi railways. The southern line is a north-south rail transport line, including the Taiyuan-Jiaozuo and Houma-Yueshan railways, which mainly transport coal to Hunan and Hubei.

八纵八横
"Eight Vertical Lines and Eight Horizontal Lines"

The rail transport network of China has taken shape in the

form of "eight vertical lines and eight horizontal lines" (vertical being south-to-north, and horizontal being east-to-west). These lines, coming under the jurisdiction of 16 railway organizations, account for 43 percent of the national total length of railways in service, but bear about 80 percent of the national total volume of passenger and freight transport, and thus are the main force in China's transportation sector. During the Tenth Five-Year Plan period (2001-2005), the Ministry of Railway strengthened the framework of the rail network, with newly built single or double-track lines and electrified lines totaling nearly 3,000 km each year.

The "eight vertical lines" are the Beijing-Harbin line (Beijing-Harbin-<Manzhouli>), coastal line (Shenyang-Dalian-Yantai-Wuxi-<Shanghai>-Hangzhou-Ningbo-Wenzhou-Xiamen-Guangzhou-<Zhanjiang>), Beijing-Shanghai line (Beijing-Shanghai), Beijing-Kowloon line (Beijing-Nanchang-Shenzhen-Kowloon), Beijing-Guangzhou line (Beijing-Wuhan-Guangzhou), Datong-Zhanjiang line (Datong-Taiyuan-Jiaozuo-Luoyang-Shimen-Yiyang-Yongzhou-Liuzhou-Zhanjiang-<Haikou>), Baotou-Liuzhou line (Baotou-Xi'an-Chongqing-Guiyang-Liuzhou-<Nanning>) and Lanzhou-Kunming line (Lanzhou-Chengdu-Kunming). The "eight horizontal lines" are the Beijing-Lanzhou line (Beijing-Hohhot-Lanzhou-<Lhasa>), northern line for coal transport (Datong-Qinhuangdao, Shenchi-Huanghua), southern line for coal transport (Taiyuan-Dezhou, Changzhi-Jinan-Qingdao, Houma-Yueshan-Xinxiang-Yanzhou-Rizhao), Luqiao line (Lianyungang-Lanzhou-Urumqi-Alashankou), Xi'an-Nanjing line (Xi'an-Nanjing-<Qidong>), Yangtze line (Chongqing-Wuhan-Jiujiang-Wuhu-Nanjing-Shanghai), Shanghai-Kunming line (Shanghai-Zhuzhou-Huaihua-Guiyang-Kunming-<Huaihua-Chongqing-Chengdu>) and the southwestern sea-bound line (Kunming-Nanning-Litang-Zhanjiang).

京沪高速铁路

Beijing-Shanghai High-speed Railway

The Beijing-Shanghai High-speed Railway is a project with the most investment and technology content in the Medium- and Long-term Program for the Railway Network approved by the State Council in early 2004. It is the first high-speed railway meeting advanced international standards in China. It runs 1,318 km, almost parallel to the existing Beijing-Shanghai Railway. In the future, the Beijing-Shanghai High-speed Railway will be used specially for passenger transport, while the Beijing-Shanghai Railway will be used mainly for freight transport. The Beijing-Shanghai High-speed Railway is a double-track one with a planned speed of 350 kph, and 300 kph during the earlier period of its service. The line will have 21 stations when it is completed and put into operation in 2010. By that time, it will take only five hours from Beijing to Shanghai (about nine hours shorter than the present journey) and it will carry 80 million passengers each way a year. Moreover, the trains leave at short intervals, with one train running every three minutes during peak time.

The Beijing-Shanghai High-speed Railway will use high-speed wheel track technology, over 70 percent of which has been developed by China itself. According to the Medium- and Long-term Program for the Railway Network, by 2020 the length of railway lines in service will have increased from 73,000 km at the end of 2003 to 100,000 km. Busy arteries will have separate passenger and freight lines, and double-track and electric railways will reach 50 percent of the total.

青藏铁路

Qinghai-Tibet Railway

The Qinghai-Tibet railway, the world's highest, started operation on July 1, 2006.

The Qinghai-Tibet Railway has the highest elevation and longest plateau length in the world. It stretches 1,956 km from Xining to Lhasa. The 814-km Xining-Golmud section was finished in 1979, and put into operation in 1984. Work started on the 1,142-km-long Golmud-Lhasa section in June 2001. Some 550 km of this section runs through permafrost and 960 km of the line is over 4,000 m above sea level, with the highest point being 5,072 m above sea level on the Tanggula Mountains. The engineers and workers successfully tackled three thorny problems—permafrost, shortage of oxygen and a fragile ecosystem. The Qinghai-Tibet Railway was linked up in October 2005, and put into trial operation on July 1, 2006.

The completion of the Qinghai-Tibet Railway was voted one of the top 10 scientific and technological achievements in 2005 by the 570 academicians of the Chinese Academy of Sciences and the Chinese Academy of Engineering. Tibet has become a new hot destination for tourists. And the scenic area along the Qinghai-Tibet Railway has been listed as a key area for priority planning and development in the 11th Five-Year Plan period (2006-2010) for China's tourism. The railway brings great opportunities for the economic development of Qinghai and Tibet, and will promote the frontier trade between Tibet and Nepal and India, gradually making the former the frontier for economic exchanges in South Asia and helping to bring into being a South Asian trade passage.

四大银行

Four Largest Banks

China's Four Largest Banks are the Industrial and Commercial Bank of China, Bank of China, China Construction Bank and Agriculture Bank of China, symbolized by a peony, the Great Wall, a dragon and a golden ear of grain, respectively.

The Industrial and Commercial Bank of China (ICBC), the largest corporate and private banking service provider in China,

The Agricultural Bank of China is one of China's four commercial banks.

supports the development of many capital construction projects and fundamental industries, key programs and enterprises, and medium and small enterprises. Since 1999 ICBC has been on the *Fortune* Global 500 list every year. In October 2005 ICBC changed from being a State-owned commercial bank into a joint-stock corporation. On October 27, 2006 ICBC Ltd was listed on the stock market in Shanghai and Hong Kong, and became the world's largest Initial Public Offering (IPO) so far by raising a total of US$ 19.1 billion through the issuance of both the A share and H share.

The Bank of China (BOC) Ltd engages in commercial banking, investment banking and insurance, and owns predominantly shares in BOC Hong Kong, BOC International, BOC Group Insurance and other financial institutions, providing personal and corporate banking services worldwide. In 2005 BOC ranked 18th in terms of core capital among the Top 1,000 World Banks by *The Banker* magazine of the UK. In July 2004, BOC became the only banking partner of the 2008 Beijing Olympic Games. In July 2006 BOC was listed on the Shanghai Stock Exchange.

The history of the China Construction Bank (CCB) dates back to October 1, 1954, when the People's Construction Bank of China was founded. This entity was renamed China Construction Bank on March 26, 1996. The CCB changed from being a State-owned commercial bank into the State-holding China Construction Bank Corporation.

The Agricultural Bank of China (ABC), with a service network covering both the urban and rural areas of China, is a large State-owned commercial bank. It boasts the most service outlets and widest service network among the country's four largest banks. Its business has expanded from rural credit and settlement to a complete range of domestic and international financial services.

人民币汇改

Reform of the RMB Exchange Rate Mechanism

The headquarters of the People's Bank of China

Before 2005 the RMB was pegged to the US dollar. Aimed at establishing and perfecting a socialist market economy and giving full play to the fundamental role of the market in resources allocation, the State Council gave approval for the practice of a controlled floating exchange rate mechanism based on market supply and demand with reference to a basket of currencies, from July 21, 2005. A basket of major currencies is a composite unit consisting of weighted amounts of the currencies in accordance with the actual development of China's international economy. The People's Bank of China announces the closing price of a foreign currency such as the US dollar traded against the RMB in the inter-bank foreign exchange market after the closing of the market on each working day, and makes it the central parity for trading against the RMB on the following working day. The daily trading price of the US dollar against the RMB on the inter-bank foreign exchange market will continue to be allowed to float within a margin of 0.3 percent around the central parity published by the People's Bank of China, while the trading prices of non-US dollar currencies against the RMB will be allowed to move within a certain margin announced by the People's Bank of China.

The People's Bank of China will adjust the RMB exchange rate margin when necessary, in accordance with the market development as well as the economic and financial situation. The RMB exchange rate will be more flexible, based on market conditions, with reference to the basket of currencies. The People's Bank of China ensures the RMB exchange rate is basically stable at an reasonable and equilibrium level.

三金工程

Three Golden Projects

At the end of 1993 China took a preliminary step toward the informationization of the national economy by formally initiating the Three Golden Projects, namely, the Golden Bridge Project, the Golden Customs Project and the Golden Card Project. The three key projects are aimed at building China's national information highway.

The Golden Bridge Project, also known as the State Public

Economic Information Network Project, is aimed at establishing a backbone network of public economic information, covering 400 cities in all the provinces (autonomous regions and municipalities directly under the central government) of China, and connects public postal and telecommunications services, radio and television, and other special communications networks. The backbone network also serves as a communications platform for other applications projects across the country.

The Golden Customs Project, also called the State International Economic and Trade Information Network Project, is aimed at advancing the replacement of the traditional way of customs declaration with electronic methods to save time and the cost of delivering documents. The network consists of two crucial systems: clearance at the office and electronic law enforcement at the port.

The Golden Card Projects, or Bank and Credit Card Payment System Project, is aimed at setting up a card application system targeted at developing and popularizing electronic currency. In January 2002 cards with the unified logo "银联 (Unionpay)" were first issued in Beijing, Shanghai and other cities. In March 2002 China Unionpay Co., Ltd, the union for developing domestic bank cards, was founded in Shanghai.

金保工程

Golden Security Project

In August 2003 the Golden Security Project was officially launched. It is a nationwide project, supporting e-governance in the handling of labor and social security affairs, provision of public services, fund supervision and management, and macro decision-making with the aid of advanced information technologies and networks at the central, provincial and city levels. The networks will take five years to construct.

The Golden Security Project will be a key to the informationization of labor security and record the payment, and manage and serve for the whole life of every insurant.

中国联通
China Unicom

China Unicom Ltd, founded on July 19, 1994 with approval from the State Council, is a comprehensive telecommunications enterprise. It was listed in Hong Kong, New York and Shanghai on June 21, 2000, June 22, 2000 and October 9, 2002, respectively. The enterprise provides services for the mobile communications of two systems, GSM and CDMA, value-added telecommunications, domestic and international long-distance calls, local calls within approval scope, data communications and Internet, and VoIP（Voice over Internet protocol）calls. As a State-owned mainstay enterprise, China Unicom has branches all over China. Its logo is derived from the ancient Chinese auspicious knot design.

China Unicom has established a nationwide communications network using advanced technologies and connected with the whole world. It boasts the second-largest user group of the CDMA system and the third-largest user group of mobile communications services in the world. This comprehensive telecommunications enterprise has both domestic and international financing channels, receives supervision from capital markets at home and abroad, and exercises management in line with the modern enterprise system and international norms. As an internationally influential telecom carrier, China Unicom was once on the *Forbes* list of global top 500 enterprises.

中国移动
China Mobile

China Mobile Communications Corporation ("China Mobile" for short) is a State-owned mainstay enterprise set up on April 20, 2000 as part of China's reform of its telecommunications system. China Mobile fully holds the equity of China Mobile (Hong Kong) Group Ltd. China Mobile Co. Ltd., in which China Mobile has majority stakes, has set up subsidiaries of its holding all over China, and has gone public on the Hong Kong and New York stock exchanges. Currently, in terms of market value, China Mobile is one of the largest of all the overseas-listed Chinese companies and of all the telecom carriers in Asia.

China Mobile operates mobile voice, data, VoIP call and multimedia services. It is well known for its brands like Go Tone, Easy-own and M-zone, and provides services through the network numbers 139, 138, 137, 136, 135, 134 (0-8) and 159. China Mobile ranks first in the world in terms of network scale and customer base. By the end of 2005, all China's counties (cites) had been covered by its network, with seamless coverage of traffic arteries and indoor coverage in key urban areas. At the same time its total number of customers had exceeded 240 million. Being included in the *Fortune* Top 500 for five consecutive yeas, China Mobile's latest ranking is 224th. It was rated fourth and second among China's Top 500 Enterprises in terms of overall strength and service provision, respectively, by the China Enterprise Confederation and China Enterprise Directors Association in 2005.

魅力城市

Charm City

Charm City is a large-scale program sponsored by China Central Television (CCTV). The program is intended to display the achievements of China's urban development, encourage creativity and individuality in urban construction, and facilitate the healthy progress of China's urbanization. In 2002 the 16th National Congress of the Communist Party of China put forth new objectives for China's urban development, namely gradually enhancing the urbanization level, maintaining coordinated development between large, medium and small cities and townships, and persisting in the road to urbanization with Chinese characteristics. To be a "Charm City" requires, above all, healthy development. And its charms can be time-honored history and culture, beautiful urban scenery, or unique folk customs, as well as a dynamic economy or uplifting ethos, or creative city construction. Furthermore, its charms should be demonstrated by representative figures and events.

Apart from the TV program, the World Union of VIP Enterprises (WUVE), US-China Economic Trade & Investment General Chamber of Commerce (USCGC) and Chinafamousbrand.com cooperate in working out the list of Top 200 Charm Cities with Chinese Characteristics. The list is aimed at enabling the world to learn more about the charms of cities with Chinese characteristics, and expand investment and cooperation between China and the rest of the world at all levels and in all fields. The 2006 list is the second comprehensive evaluation of the more than 600 cities on China's mainland, and Hong Kong, Macao and Taiwan by the World-famous Brand Assembly (WFBA). The vital standard for charm is Chinese characteristics in lifestyle, history, ecology and production.

百强城市

China's Top 100 Cities in terms of Comprehensive Strength

The selection of China's Top 100 Cities in terms of Comprehensive Strength sponsored by the National Bureau of Statistics of China is an all-round evaluation of the comprehensive strength of Chinese cities at and above the prefecture level. The indices of cities' comprehensive strength are utilization of population and labor resources, economic development, social development, infrastructure, environmental protection and a recycling economy. The top ten cities on the 2005 list were Shanghai, Beijing, Shenzhen, Guangzhou, Tianjin, Dalian, Nanjing, Hangzhou, Shenyang and Harbin. The National Bureau of Statistics also surveys China's Top 50 Cities in terms of investment environment, focusing on human resources, social services, economy, comprehensive security, infrastructure, geographic location, natural environment and market. The first ten cities on the 2005 list in this regard were Beijing, Tianjin, Tangshan, Qinhuangdao, Taiyuan, Hohhot, Baotou, Shenyang, Dalian and Changchun, in sequence.

In October 2005, the China Urban Economy Society initiated the first assessment of China's urban tourism competitiveness, and 173 renowned tourist cities, including Beijing, Shanghai, Shenzhen, Guangzhou and Hangzhou, registered for the activity. Urban tourism competitiveness refers to the comprehensive capability and quality of a city in creating and developing its tourism environment, expanding its tourism market, and tourism management and innovation. When the result was released in November 2006 the first ten on the list of China's Top 100 Cities in terms of Tourism Competitiveness were Guangzhou,

Shenzhen, Hangzhou, Chengdu, Nanjing, Suzhou, Dalian, Qingdao, Wuxi and Ningbo, in sequence.

数字城市

Digital City

The concept of "Digital City" originates from the idea of "Digital Earth" set forth by former US Vice-president Al Gore in 1998. Digital City is a technological system that integrates information on urban planning, construction, management, production and standard of living by dint of information processing and network communication technologies, such as Geographic Information System (GIS), Global Positioning System (GPS) and Remote Sensing (RS). It automatically collects information, and dynamically monitors and controls, and assists decision-making regarding urban infrastructure and functional mechanisms. Digital City turns the complex geographical and ecological environment, and social environment, including population and traffic, into a digital and visual network.

It is estimated that China's urbanization rate will reach 40 percent by 2010, and 50 to 52 percent by 2020. As the process of urbanization speeds up, more urban communities take shape and traffic grows congested with each passing day, the need for network management and dynamic control becomes increasingly imperative. Digital City has plenty of scope for application. During the 10th Five-Year Plan Period (2001-2005), under the new circumstances of economic globalization and China's entry into the WTO, huge amounts of capital were channeled into research for China's Digital Zone projects at all levels, including Digital Industry, Digital Province, Digital City, and Digital Community. In October 2006, China's State Bureau of Surveying and Mapping and State Council Informationization Office announced their guidelines for strengthening the Digital China geo-spatial framework construction and application services. The plan is aimed at basically completing the data system of the Digital China geo-spatial framework by 2010. The Digital Zone geo-spatial framework, including Digital Province and Digital City, is an organic component of the Digital China geo-spatial framework.

广交会

Canton Fair

In 1956 the Bureau of Foreign Trade of Guangdong Province proposed to the central government that a national export exposition be held in Guangzhou. In November of the same year the two-month China Export Exposition was officially inaugurated in Guangzhou. Nearly 10,000 of China's major export items at the time were on show at the Exposition, and the Chinese trading delegations concluded deals with over 5,000 buyers from dozens of countries and regions, involving a total turnover of US$ 50 million. In 1957 the Chinese government decided to hold the China Export Exposition, also called the Canton Fair, in Guangzhou twice a year, in spring and autumn. The Canton Fair has continued for over half a century, and the year 2006 witnessed its 100th session. Today it has become a comprehensive international trade event for China with the longest history, the largest scale, the biggest variety of exhibits, the largest number of buyers and the highest turnover.

The 100th session of China Export Exposition held from October 15 to 30, 2006 received 14,000 enterprises and nearly 500,000 buyers, the largest scale ever in its history. That session achieved a record turnover of US$ 34.06 billion. The EU, the

US and the Middle East, with US$11.59 billion, US$5.01 billion and US$4.06 billion, respectively, were the three biggest buyers. To better cope with the new circumstances of reform and opening-up, expand imports and exports, and foster the coordinated and balanced development of import and export trade, the Chinese government decided to rename the Canton Fair the China Import and Export Fair from its 101st session.

A foreign businessman examines a sample during the 100th China Import and Export Fair held in Guangzhou in 2006.

物权法

Real Estate Rights Law

The Real Estate Rights Law of the People's Republic of China was adopted at the Fifth Session of the 10th National

People's Congress on March 16, 2007, and went into effect on October 1, 2007. The Real Estate Rights Law is a basic civil law that regulates property relationships and adjusts civil relationships incurred from the attribution and utilization of real estate, including clearly defining the real estate rights of the State, collective, individual or any other real estate rights holder, and the protection of these rights. The Law was first drafted in the early 1990s. The National People's Congress examined and discussed the draft seven times, the most times it has ever done so for a draft law, and announced the full text of the draft in July 2005 to solicit the opinions of people of all walks of life. Responding to the requirements of deepening reform, wider opening-up, developing economic, political, cultural and social construction, the Real Estate Rights Law lays down rules for solving the common problems regarding the real estate rights system and other problems that urgently need to be solved.

The Law is divided into five parts, namely, General Rules, Ownership, Usufructuary Right, Security and Possession, comprising 247 articles. According to the Law, the public economy shall be consolidated and developed by the State, and the development of the non-public economy shall be encouraged, supported and guided. The Real Estate Rights Law clearly defines property owned by the State and intensifies the protection of property owned by the State in five aspects. To grant farmers long-term and guaranteed rights to the use of land, the Law stipulates that after the contractual term of cultivated land, grassland or woodland expires, the holder of the right to the contracted management of the land may, in accordance with the relevant provisions of the State, continue to contract the land. It proclaims that an individual's legal property shall be protected by law, and no entity or individual may encroach upon it. The Real Estate Rights Law was drawn up in line with the requirement of adhering to the basic socialist economic system, regulating the order of the socialist market economy, and safeguarding the immediate interests of the broad masses of the people. As an indispensable major law, it plays a supporting role in the socialist legal system with Chinese characteristics.

京津冀都市圈

Beijing-Tianjin-Hebei Metropolitan Region

The Beijing-Tianjin-Hebei (BTH) Metropolitan Region, consisting of Beijing and Tianjin, two municipalities directly under the central government, and some cities in the surrounding Hebei Province, is considered a new source of economic growth after the Zhujiang River and Yangtze River delta regions.

The BTH Region is home to several of China's leading industries. Its new and high-tech industries include electronic information, bio-pharmaceuticals, and finance and insurance, business and information, and conference and exhibition services. Modern manufacturing industries in the region include automobile manufacturing and pharmaceuticals, and its iron and steel, and petrochemical industries are playing a conspicuous supporting role in the national economic development. The Beijing-Tianjin-Tanggu Belt of new and high-tech industries, and a clutch of modern manufacturing industries along the Beijing-Shijiazhuang Expressway have taken initial shape. The adjustments in the State's industrial macro-policies will expedite the trend of industrial agglomeration in some advantageously located areas of the BTH region, and facilitate fundamental changes in industrial development and agglomeration in some other areas as a result of the transformation of their economic functions. In the next 10 to 20 years, China as a whole will be at the intermediate phase of industrialization, and it is expected that the BTH Region will surpass the national average and reach the advanced phase of industrialization by 2020. The Region is roughly at the primary stage of the intermediate phase, and Beijing is moving from the intermediate to the advanced phase. Therefore, promoting modern manufacturing industries, increasing the proportion of new and high-tech industries, updating traditional chemical industries and promoting modern service industries are the focuses of industrial development of the BTH Region.

A general industrial division has taken shape among cities in the BTH Region, each choosing and developing industries in which they have an advantage. Beijing's industrial development is led by new and high-tech industries, especially the manufacturing of communication equipment, computers and other electronic devices, and transportation equipment; Tianjin has a complete industrial system characterized by attaching parallel importance to new and high-tech industries, such as the manufacturing of communications equipment, computers and other electronic devices, and heavy industries, including petroleum, chemicals and metallurgy. The industrial development of the cities in Hebei Province such as Shijiazhuang, Baoding, Tangshan, Qinhuangdao, Langfang, Cangzhou, Zhangjiakou, Chengde, Handan, Hengshui and Xingtai focuses on the mining and processing of coal and ferrous metals, exploitation of petroleum and natural gas, agricultural product processing industries and beverage manufacturing.

农业 农村 农民

Agriculture, Rural Areas and Farmers

三农问题

Issue of Agriculture, Rural Areas and Farmers

The issue of agriculture, rural areas and farmers was first put forward by Dr Wen Tiejun in 1996. In 2003, the Chinese government officially listed the issue in the Report on the Work of the Government, and the issue has remained a priority on the government agenda.

In 2006, the work of the government related to agriculture, rural areas and farmers was intensified, and steady progress was made in building a new socialist countryside, according to the Report on the Work of the Government delivered by Premier Wen Jiabao at the Fifth Session of the 10th National People's Congress on March 5, 2007. In 2006, central government budgetary spending on agriculture, rural areas and farmers reached 339.7 billion yuan, an increase of 42.2 billion yuan compared to the previous year. At the same time, the agricultural tax and taxes on special agricultural products were rescinded nationwide. The government continued to increase direct subsidies to grain farmers, and subsidies to farmers for growing superior seeds and purchasing agricultural machinery and tools, and followed a policy of granting general subsidies for agricultural production supplies. In addition, the government continued the guaranteed minimum purchase price policy for major grains in main grain-producing areas, and increased transfer payments to counties and townships with financial difficulties. Despite serious natural disasters, the output of major agricultural products increased steadily. In 2006, the grain output reached 497.46 million tons, registering the third consecutive annual increase. The government worked harder to develop rural infrastructure, including roads, water conservancy projects, electricity and communications, and made safe drinking water available to another 28.97 million rural residents and the use of methane available to an additional 4.5 million rural households, thereby improving working and living conditions in rural areas. Continued progress was recorded in reducing rural poverty through development, lifting 2.17 million rural people out of poverty. Meanwhile, the government formulated and implemented policies and measures to address the difficulties faced by migrant workers in cities, and strengthened the protection of their legitimate rights and interests by addressing the problems of low wages and unpaid wages, standardizing labor management pursuant to the law, improving job training and expanding social security.

农业普查

Agricultural Census

A census covering agriculture is carried out every ten years in China, starting in 1996. The 2006 census covered over 200 million rural families belonging to more than 600,000 villagers' committees of 30,000 townships. With more than seven million census takers, it was the biggest project of its kind ever conducted in the world.

The purposes of the agricultural census are to acquire basic information about China's agriculture, rural areas and farmers, to lay a foundation for studying and making social economic development plans, strategies, policies and scientific decisions, and to provide statistics to farmers and the public. The census targets rural households, both farming households and others, township farming households, farming enterprises, villagers' committees and people's governments at township level. The economic activities surveyed are crop planting, forestry, animal husbandry and fisheries, and their related service trades, including agricultural production conditions, farming activities, utilization of farmland, rural labor and employment, infrastructure facilities in rural areas, social services in rural areas and farmers' living standards, as well as villagers' and residents' committees and community environment.

现代农业
Modern Agriculture

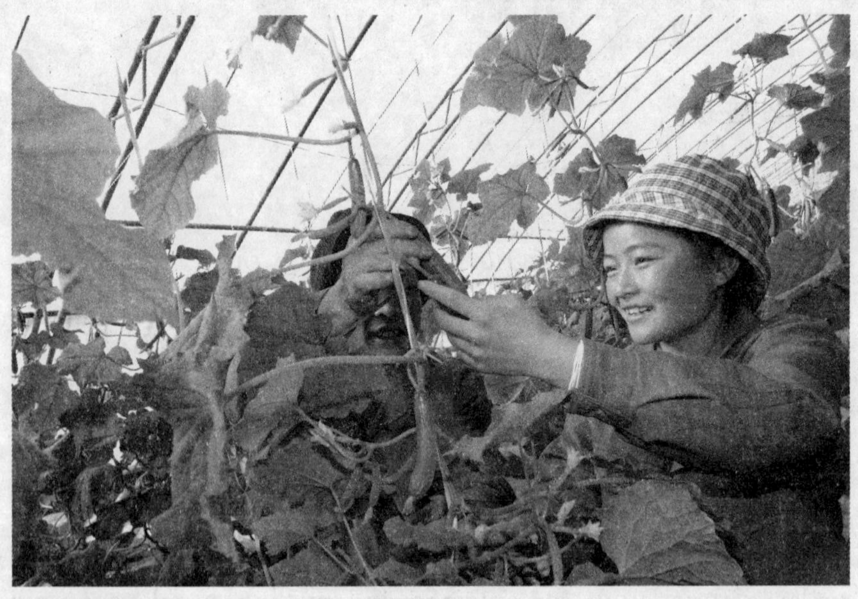

Vegetable growers work in a modern greenhouse.

At present, China's agriculture is in a transitional period, with modern agriculture replacing traditional agriculture. Taking scientific and technological innovation as an example: China's transfer rate of scientific and technological achievements into agricultural production is 48 percent, nearly 30 percentage points lower than in developed countries. This shows that China's potential for extending the application of agricultural science and technology to enhance agricultural production is high. Even ordinary technologies can have obvious effects on productivity if they are put to practical use. The work of putting agricultural science and technology to practical use, launched in 2004, had been extended to 212 counties by 2006. A new breakthrough in super-rice breeding technology has attained the level of 12,000 kg per ha, leading the "third revolution in rice production."

The Ministry of Agriculture has put forward a scheme which distributes advantageous agricultural products by region, aiming to set up a group of zones specializing in these products and spurring the industrialization of agriculture. The processing rate of China's agricultural products reached 30 percent during the Tenth Five-Year Plan period (2001-2005). In the guidelines of the 11th Five-Year Plan, the main plan to develop modern agriculture entails increasing production through structural adjustment, better services and improved circulation systems in rural areas.

免征农业税

Rescinding the Agricultural Tax

The agricultural tax, which had been levied for 2,600 years in China, targeted all units and individuals involved in farm production or having income from agriculture. The Chinese government introduced the policy of reducing the agricultural tax and exempting certain people from it in 2004. In March

2005, Premier Wen Jiabao announced that the agricultural tax would be reduced nationwide, exempting 592 counties on the list of "National Program for Reducing Rural Poverty through Development" from the agricultural and animal husbandry taxes. The decrease in agricultural revenue would be filled by special transfer payments from the central government. At the end of 2005, farmers in 28 provinces and 210 counties in Hebei, Shandong and Yunnan provinces were exempted from the agricultural tax.

The 19th session of the Standing Committee of the Tenth National People's Congress, held in December 2005, revoked the regulation on levying agricultural tax nationwide from 2006, saving for the country's 900 million farmers a total of over 100 billion yuan every year (120 yuan per person, on average). In addition, since 2003, the Chinese government has issued a series of policies which increase agricultural subsidies, and thereby benefiting the farmers.

农业钟点工
Agricultural Part-time Workers

At present, many farmers form working teams to provide part-time labor for short-handed families in rural areas, which satisfies the need of some major grain and livestock producers for labor and at the same time increases the teams' income. With the recent progress in agricultural technologies, skilled hands can earn 3.5 to 4 yuan per hour, which is about 30 to 40 yuan a day. Agricultural part-time workers include not only farmers, but also some unemployed and laid-off workers living in towns and cities.

In addition, new agricultural organizations and agricultural enterprises also provide some agricultural service posts. Young people in rural areas, after being trained in agricultural skills, can engage in seasonal agricultural services like pruning fruit trees, preventing and controlling plant diseases and eliminating pests, and packing and marketing agricultural products. Some services are paid by the piece, some by the hour and some monthly. These newly-emerged services can both solve the problem of labor shortages in the production and sale seasons of agricultural products, and create more jobs for young people in rural areas. With the benefits of the accelerating urbanization process in the rural areas and the constantly improving land-transfer system, it is expected that there will be more and more part-time jobs in rural areas.

社会主义新农村

New Socialist Countryside

In October 2005, the building of a new socialist countryside was put forward as a historic task for China at the Fifth Plenary Session of the 16th CPC Central Committee. The so-called "new socialist countryside" covers five aspects: new houses, new infrastructures, new environment, new farmers and new customs. The goals are "advanced production, well-off living standard, healthy rural customs, neat and clean villages, and democratic management."

There are over 600,000 administrative villages and three million natural villages throughout China, with a big difference in their natural, economic and cultural conditions. The primary step in building a new socialist countryside is the enhancement of rural productivity. The government is trying to change the development mode of agriculture, and improve its comprehensive production and value-adding abilities. Starting by solving the most urgent problems and those of most serious concern to the farmers, the government is stressing the continuous increases of farmers' income. In addition, the government keeps tapping the potential within agriculture and expanding the scope both within and outside the countryside for the farmers to increase their income. The second step is to improve infrastructural construction in the rural areas. The government aims to strengthen capital construction in farming areas with small irrigation facilities as the key projects, providing adequate water, roads, electricity and gas, solving the pollution problem and improving the farmers' living conditions. The third step is to develop public services such as education, medical care and culture in rural areas. With funds from the public budget, nine-year compulsory education will be further consolidated in the rural areas. The three-level healthcare services and medical assistance system will be strengthened through enlarging the coverage of rural cooperative medical services and providing more subsidies. More cultural installations will be set up in rural areas to enrich the farmers' cultural life.

文明生态村

Eco-villages

In early 2005, a working meeting for the development of cultural life in China's rural areas held in Hainan Province by the Publicity Department of CCCPC (Central Committee of the Communist Party of China) and the Civilization Administrative Office of the CCCPC called the province's eco-village construction project "a new road to building harmonious villages." By February 2006, over 5,200 eco-villages, accounting for 22 percent of the total natural villages in Hainan, had been built. Since 2001, the Hainan government has drawn up and publicized a series of specific standards and requirements for eco-villages. For example, to solve the farmers' health, lighting and fuel problems it is required that every household build a methane-generating pit and rebuild toilets, stoves and livestock pens, and purify drinking water used by people and livestock. In addition, village roads and peasants' houses must be improved, with trees planted in and around villages and yards, and every eco-village should have a sports ground, a CPC members' activity center and a library. The project envisages nine systems, including the Villagers' Public Health Pledge System.

Windmill energy is widely used in village greenhouses in the suburbs of Zhengzhou, Henan Province.

Hainan's eco-villages feature various development modes, such as the "small household, large property" mode featuring "methane gas + raising pigs + planting cash crops," and the "eco-village + specialized village" mode featuring latex, rattan and bamboo, medicinal herbs and tea as cash-earning products. Some counties (cities) integrate tourism into eco-village construction, gaining good ecological and economic benefits from eco-tourism programs.

新型农民

New-type Farmer

A "Happy Farmer Cup" watermelon contest was held in Haikou of Hainan Province in the purpose of popularizing science and fostering new farmers.

A new-type farmer should have the following qualities: Firstly, he or she should be literate, independent and trustworthy, and should support the role of science and technology in the rural areas and know and abide by the law. Secondly, he or she should be "skilled," with a technological background and having mastered at least one production skill. In addition, he or she should possess business skills, such as knowing how to properly allocate human, capital, material and land resources, organize production, engage in market activities, and gain benefits as a result.

At present, among the 490-million-strong rural labor force nationwide, only 13 percent have received a senior high school education, and 49 percent a junior high school education, while the other 38 percent have only a primary school education (of whom seven percentage points are illiterate). During the 11th Five-Year Plan period (2006-2010), China will accelerate the development of education, vocational training and cultural undertakings in the rural areas in order to cultivate educated and skilled farmers who are able to run businesses. In 2006, the central budget earmarked 100 million yuan for the "Science and Technology Training Program for Farmers" in 10,000 selected villages. Each village got a subsidy of 10,000 yuan to provide farmers with vocational training. It is estimated that by 2010 some 100 million farmers will receive systematic training under the program, among whom 50 million will receive training in agricultural technology and the other 50 million will be trained for skills required for new posts.

农民增收

Increasing Rural Income

The government "needs to implement a policy of getting industry to support agriculture and cities to support the countryside, strengthen support for agriculture, rural areas and farmers, and continue making reforms in rural systems and innovations in rural institutions to bring about a rapid and significant change in the overall appearance of the countryside," said Premier Wen Jiabao in the Report on the Work of the Government delivered at the Fourth Session of the Tenth National People's Congress on March 5, 2006. During the Tenth Five-Year Plan period (2001-2005), the annual increase of per capita net income in the countryside averaged 5.3 percent. In 2006, the average net income for each farmer was 3,587 yuan, an increase of 7.4 percent over 2005 after adjusting for inflation. The sources of rural income also saw some significant changes: The income from growing food crops and raising livestock went up rapidly, as did transfer income and salary income. The service industry became a new growth point for rural income. The rural income rose especially in major grain-production areas.

According to the index standards for a well-off society published by the National Bureau of Statistics, per capita net income in rural areas should reach 8,000 yuan by 2020, meaning an average annual increase of 6.8 percent in the years leading to 2020. However, in the past two decades, the annual increase of rural per capita net income averaged below four percent, and even lower in the central and western areas. To increase rural income during the 11th Five-Year Plan period (2006-2010), besides tapping the potential for increasing agricultural production and increasing farmers' income from nonagricultural sectors, the Chinese government will also improve the policies for reducing the burden on farmers, including continuing to increase direct subsidies to them and improving the subsidy channels, keeping the prices of agricultural products stable, improving the supply of materials needed for agricultural production, establishing a supportive and protective system for agriculture, strictly controlling agricultural charges, and prohibiting arbitrary charges and unchecked apportioning of tasks.

脱贫
Out-of-Poverty Campaign

Accompanying the progress of the reform and opening-up policies since the end of the 1970s, the Chinese government has conducted a well-organized Out-of-Poverty Campaign that focuses on solving the problem of food and clothing of the poverty-stricken populace. In 2005, the population without adequate food and clothing in rural areas was 23.65 million, compared to 250 million in 1978. According to statistics from the State Council's Poverty Alleviation and Development Office, the net decrease in the rural poor population averaged 13.5 million per year during the 1980s and 5.3 million per year during the 1990s, while the number shrank to only 1.3 million per year from 2001 to 2005. The poverty-stricken populace are now mainly distributed in areas with poor natural conditions, so it becomes harder and costs much more to lift them out of poverty. The Ministry of Agriculture plans to conduct experiments in 30 poor counties nationwide varying in development levels and modes, as examples for the construction of a "new countryside" and poverty alleviation.

In addition, the emphasis of China's infrastructure construction will turn to the countryside. The Chinese government will establish a relatively complete public health and basic medical system, an aid system for fundamental education and a social security system, and gradually provide the same public services to all people in both rural and urban areas. These measures will benefit the poverty-stricken populace in outlying areas.

广播电视村村通工程
"Broadcast to Every Village" Program

Since the State initiated the "Broadcast to Every Village" program in 1998, radio and television broadcasts have become available to 100 million more farmers. By 2003, all administrative villages with power supply could receive radio and television signals, and by 2006, all natural villages with power supply having over 50 households could receive radio and television signals. The comprehensive coverage of radio and television had increased to 94.48 percent and 95.81 percent, respectively, in 2005, compared to 86.02 percent and 87.68 percent in 1997.

However, in general, China's rural broadcasting is not satisfactory. Some areas are not covered by the broadcasting network, and some areas can only receive a few low-quality programs. According to a report by the State Council, by the end of 2010 radio and television coverage will reach every natural village with power supply having over 20 households.

农村电影放映工程

Rural Film Projection Program

The Rural Film Projection Program was initiated by the State Administration of Radio, Film and Television, Ministry of Culture, National Development and Reform Commission and Ministry of Finance in 1998. During the Tenth Five-Year Plan period (2001-2005), over 35,000 rural film projection teams were organized, and showed films all over the country on more than 20 million occasions. During the 11th Five-Year Plan period (2006-2010), the administration departments of radio, film and television are scheduled to develop digital film projection in rural areas, whereby feature and educational films will be directly sent to the projection locations via digital signals. The Rural Film Projection Program plans to show at least one film a month in all rural communities by 2010.

Besides the "Broadcast to Every Village" program and the Rural Film Projection Program, there is also the Tibet-Xinjiang Program set up to improve the broadcasting infrastructure in those two autonomous regions.

新型农村合作医疗制度

New Rural Cooperative Medical System

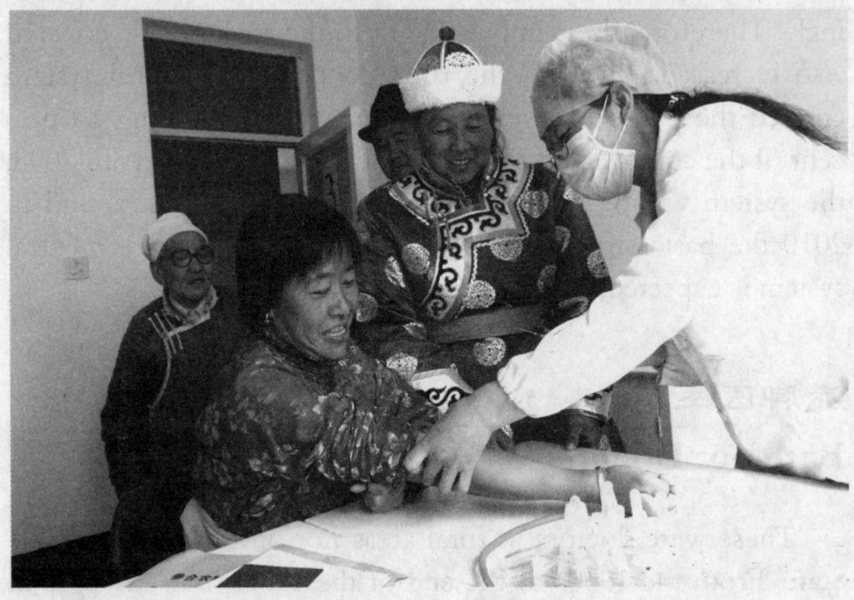

Farmers who have joined the new-type rural cooperative medical care system are having physical checks.

In 2003 China began to establish a new rural cooperative medical system. This medical system, mainly covering major illnesses, collects funds from three sources: personal payment, collective aid and government investment. Joining the system is voluntary, and each member pays ten yuan into the fund, while the province, city and county fiscal authorities together pay another ten yuan, and the central government pays a further ten yuan. In 2006, the contributions from the two government sources was raised to 20 yuan per person in the central and western rural areas.

In 2006, a total of 1,451 counties (cities and districts) participated in the trial of this medical system, accounting for 50.7 percent of China's total and covering 410 million farmers. The central finance paid 4.27 billion yuan in that year, and the expenditure by the local fiscal authorities increased correspondingly. Therefore, the reimbursement to the rural people covered also increased. In 2007, the rural cooperative medical system entered the phase of overall implementation, covering 80 percent of the counties (cities and districts) of the country. In 2008, the system will be spread to cover the whole country, and in 2010 the basic structure of the new rural cooperative medical system is expected to be in place.

赤脚医生

Barefoot Doctors

These were doctors in rural areas not on the payroll of the State. From the 1950s to the end of the 1980s, most villages in China had barefoot doctors, as there was a lack of professional doctors during that period. The barefoot doctors were trained to meet the emergency needs of medical care in rural areas. They could only treat minor ailments like fevers and less-severe injuries. They had no regular income. But the Administrative Bylaws Concerning Rural Doctors, published January 1, 2004, stipulates that only after being registered and certificated are barefoot doctors allowed to provide medical services like preventive health care and general medical treatment at the village level. And only those who have passed an examination or have 20 years' medical practice get certification.

"The last barefoot doctor" Li Chunyan, who graduated from the Congjiang Professional Sanitary School, has been providing 2,500 villagers with medical services for five years. She persisted in what she was doing, although she had run into debt of a result of the job. She was appraised as the "2004 Personage of the Year" by *Nanfengchuang* magazine, and as one of the "Ten Figures that Moved China in 2005" by CCTV.

大学生村官

College-Graduate Village Officials

In 2006, Beijing launched the "Talents for Villages" project to encourage college graduates to find jobs in basic government organs in the countryside. The project aims to have a college-graduate administrator in every village in three to five years' time. On July 14, 2006, some 2,016 college graduates went to 1,853 villages on the outskirts of Beijing to work as assistants to head of villagers' committees. Beijing plans to employ about 8,000 college graduates before 2010 in this way, two for each village.

Experts point out that a new way to train and temper talented young people is to make college graduates village administrators. A great number of job opportunities in the construction of new-type villages and a series of favorable policies attract college graduates to villages through open application and voluntary employment. The traditional barriers between statuses, city and village, and regional areas are broken and college graduates will get more opportunities for employment. Furthermore, it is also a means to promote the bidirectional flow of talents between cities and countryside, and improve the construction of new-type villages.

乡镇企业

Township Enterprises

Township enterprises are those run in rural areas by farmers themselves. The reform in the rural areas and the development of agricultural technologies have liberated a large number of laborers from farming. This has provided the labor foundation for the development of township enterprises. Their products are low-priced, and sell well in cities and villages throughout China. Township enterprises are involved in a wide range of areas, including industry, agricultural product processing, communications, building industry, commerce, food and beverage industry and service trades. In 2006, China had over 23 million township enterprises with 146.52 million employees. They created 5.75 trillion yuan of added value in that year, an increase of 13.2 percent over the previous year. These enterprises have become the major source of increases in farmers' income and the rural economy as a whole. In the Yangtze and Pearl river delta areas, where township enterprises are quite developed, income from township enterprises makes up about 80 percent of the annual net income for farmers.

Over a long period of development, Chinese township enterprises have become the dominant force in the county-level economy and the most active aspect of national economic growth. Now, two-thirds of township enterprises with annual turnover of more than ten million yuan each have set up R&D centers. A group of leading enterprises with self-innovation capability and independent intellectual property rights has taken shape.

多予 少取 放活

Give More, Take Less and Liven Up

On February 8, 2004, the Opinion of the Central Committee of the Communist Party of China and the State Council on

Some Policies for Promoting the Increase of Farmers' Income, also known as the CCCPC Document No. 1 for 2004, was issued. The document emphasized that the government should adhere to the guideline of "Give More, Take Less and Liven Up" to increase farmers' incomes.

For many years, the net income of farmers nationwide rose slowly, and the rate of increase of farmers' income in the major grain-production areas has been smaller than the country's average. The earnings of many farmer families remained stagnant for years, and in some cases even decreased. Now is the period with the most abundant agricultural products supply in Chinese history, but it is also the period with the largest income gap between urban and rural residents since China's adoption of the reform and opening-up policies over 20 years ago. The task of increasing farmers' incomes is an urgent one. Experts urge an increase in investment in agriculture to enhance the infrastructure in rural areas and develop agricultural science and technology. This will provide favorable conditions for increasing farmers' incomes. This is the "Give more" part of the formula. "Take less" means, on the basis of solidifying the present efforts, the government should gradually cancel the taxes that are a burden on farmers' shoulders. The end result will be the unification of taxation in both rural and urban areas. "Liven Up" means giving farmers a free hand to invigorate the rural economy, and, through deepening the reform of the rural economic structure, to stir up the farmers' enthusiasm to start new undertakings and increase their incomes.

教育

Education

科教兴国

Revitalizing the Country Through Science and Education

A tutor from the Nanyang Museum of Science and Technology of Henan Province brought a "small robot" to the classroom of the Experiment School in Wolong District of Nanyang.

The strategy of "revitalizing the country through science and education" is a practical application of the concept that "science and technology is the primary productive force." The Chinese government has put science and technology and education in a significant position in the course of its endeavors for economic and social progress. This will increase the country's strength in science and technology and its ability to turn it into an effective productive force, and enhance the level of science and technology and culture of the whole nation. In fact, economic growth will more and more depend on progress in science and technology and the raising of workers' level of skill and all-round knowledge. The idea was first put forth in 1995 in a joint decision of the CCCPC and the State Council on accelerating the progress of science and technology. The Fourth Session of the Eighth National People's Congress, held in 1996, decided that this strategy would be a basic national policy.

This strategy links education more closely with the modernization process of the country. In recent years, China's spending on education has increased remarkably. Since 1998, the rate of educational funds in total government expenditure has seen a one-percentage-point increase every year. According to the goal set for the 11th Five-Year Plan period, the Chinese government will ensure government funding for education increase at a higher rate than that of its revenue and gradually make it account for four percent of China's GDP. Education in China is developing in both its depth and width, and international professional degrees like MBA, EMBA and MPA are now much sought after. Various types of professional tests and related training courses in subjects like computer science and foreign languages are all the rage. In addition, life-long education has become a trend.

素质教育
Essential-Quality-Oriented Education

There are two education modes in China: test-oriented and essential-quality-oriented. Test-oriented education trains students only for passing exams and entering good schools, while neglecting the needs for personal and social development. Essential-quality-oriented education, however, aims at cultivating the essential qualities required for personal and social development. It emphasizes developing a person's potential to the full, forming a complete personality and strengthening creativity and initiative.

The Outline of China's Educational Reform and Development, issued in February 1993, pointed out: "Education at the primary and middle school stages must change from being test-oriented education to education aiming at improving the qualities of our citizens in an all-round way. It must boost the comprehensive development of ethics, scientific knowledge, skills, and physical and psychological qualities, and encourage students to grow up to be active members of the society exercising initiative." From then on, China gradually changed its educational mode from test-oriented to essential-quality-oriented.

两基

Two Basic Goals for Education

These goals are making nine-year compulsory education (including primary and junior middle school education) universally available and basically wiping out illiteracy among young and middle-aged adults. By early 2007, some 2,900 county-level administrative regions had realized the two goals, accounting for 96 percent of China's total territory and 98 percent of the entire population. According to the Ministry of Education statistics, in 2006 the enrollment ratio of primary schools had reached 99.27 percent, and that of junior middle schools was 97 percent. Since the early 1990s, enrollment in primary schools has been on the decline because the school-age population shrank year by year. In 2006, however, the number rose to 17,293,600, because the enrollment in rural areas increased. The total number of students enrolled in junior middle schools (including secondary vocational schools) was 19,295,600 nationwide in that year, keeping a downward trend, but this number was larger than the number of primary school graduates. The main reasons are, according to a preliminary analysis, that the Chinese government built more boarding junior middle schools, paid tuition fees and extras for students from poor families to receive compulsory education, provided them with free textbooks and granted them living allowances. These measures greatly encouraged new primary school graduates to enter junior middle school and previous primary school graduates to go back to school. In 2006, primary school students totaled 107,115,300 nationwide, and junior middle school (including secondary vocational school) students totaled 59,579,500.

The major goals for education during the 11th Five-Year Plan (2006-2010) period are: Nine-year compulsory education will be available to 100 percent of the population; senior middle school enrollment will reach 80 percent, and the total enrolment in secondary vocational schools will be generally equal to that of ordinary senior middle schools. The enrollment ratio of institutions of higher learning will be about 25 percent, various types of vocational training and continuing education will be developed considerably. An overall study-oriented society is envisaged.

"两基"攻坚计划

Carrying Out the Two Basic Goals for Education

The central government decided to achieve the "Two Basic Goals for Education"—making compulsory education available to all children in the remote western regions and poor areas, and wiping out illiteracy among young and middle-aged people—within four years' time from 2004 to 2007. Great efforts have been made to build and equip rural boarding schools, and to complete the modern rural primary and middle school distance education project. In 2007, all areas in western China had completed the "Two Basic Goals."

At the Fifth Session of the Tenth National People's Congress, which opened March 5, 2007, Premier Wen Jiabao said in his Report on the Work of the Government: In 2006, of the 410 targeted counties, 317 reached the goals of making nine-year compulsory education available and basically eliminating illiteracy among young and middle-aged adults. The proportion of the target population attaining these two goals in the western region increased to 96 percent from 77 percent in 2003. The central government spent nine billion yuan over the past three years building and equipping 7,651 rural boarding schools. Eight billion yuan was spent on developing modern primary and middle school distance education for rural areas. The whole project covers over 80 percent of the rural primary and middle schools in the central and western regions, and enables over 100 million students to have access to high-quality education. In 2007, we would ensure that the plan to make nine-year compulsory education would generally be available and illiteracy among young and middle-aged adults would basically be eliminated in the western region, and the modern rural primary and middle school distance education project would achieve their final objectives. We would work to ensure that all children could afford to receive good education.

两免一补

Two Exemptions and One Allowance

In 2005, China initiated the policy of "Two Exemptions and One Allowance" for rural compulsory education, and began carrying it out in 592 poverty-stricken counties. "Two Exemptions" means that the government grants exemptions from tuition and miscellaneous fees, and textbook fees; "One Allowance" is a living allowance granted to boarding students. In the same year, seven billion yuan was allocated by both the central and local governments to over 34 million students from poor families. The objectives of the policy are to ensure that students from poor rural families receive compulsory education and students from poor urban families receive basic cost-of-living allowances.

In 2006, a total of 184 billion yuan was allocated by both the central and local governments to fund rural compulsory education, paying tuition and miscellaneous fees for the 52 million rural students receiving compulsory education in western China and in some areas of central China, providing free textbooks to 37.3 million students from poor families and granting living allowances to 7.8 million boarding students. In 2007, the government exempted tuition and miscellaneous fees from all rural students receiving compulsory education. This eased the financial burden of 150 million rural households with children attending primary and middle schools. The State will continue to provide free textbooks for students from poor rural families receiving compulsory education and living allowances for boarding students.

择校

Choosing Schools

During the compulsory education stage (primary and junior middle schools) in China, there is no entrance examination, and the students go to a school near their home. From junior to senior middle school, the schools choose the best from the students who take the entrance examination, adhering to the conditions prescribed by local governments. However, because of the imbalance in educational development, the scarcity of high-quality educational resources and the traditional Chinese view of elite education, there is heated competition to enter prestigious schools. Making the situation worse is the fact that top schools charge exorbitant fees, resulting in educational privileges for higher-income families.

In 2003, the State issued the "Three Restrictions." Public senior middle schools—after completing the enrollment plan of the year—may recruit a certain number of students who want to choose schools on the condition that they meet the requirement on the number of such students enrolled, the maximum amount of fees they could charge and the same mark standard for all students. The policy prescribed that the proportion of school-choosing students and the lowest school-entering mark standard should be decided by the education administrative department at provincial level, and the fees should be proposed by the education administrative department at provincial level with financial and price-fixing departments and approved by the provincial people's government. At the same time, school-choosing students should be included in the enrollment plan of senior middle schools, which should inform the public of the proportion of school-choosing students, the number of such students to be enrolled, and the fees that will be charged. The senior middle school should recruit the bests from school-choosing students according to marks, and go through the uniform procedures.

代课老师

Temporary Teachers

Temporary teachers are those teaching on a part-time basis

in rural schools but not on the government payroll. They are largely paid by the local villages, and hence were called village teachers till the end of 1984. Since 1985, rural schools have been forbidden to hire village teachers, but at the end of 2005 there were still about 448,000 temporary teachers in primary and middle schools around China. Among them, 300,000 were in public primary and middle schools in rural areas, accounting for 5.9 percent of the total number of teachers in those schools. In July 2006, the Ministry of Education announced that it would dismiss all the 448,000 temporary teachers. Those who think they have the necessary credentials and qualifications to continue the job must take part in the recruitment organized by local governments.

希望工程
Project Hope

Led by the Communist Youth League, Project Hope is a public service project initiated in October 1989 by the China Youth Development Foundation, which also organizes the project. According to China's policy of collecting educational funds from various channels, this non-governmental project has established the Project Hope Foundation funded by various sources from at home and abroad. Its goal is to support young dropouts, improve educational facilities and teaching quality, and develop fundamental education in poverty-stricken areas.

Project Hope helps to build and equip classrooms, dormitories, libraries, gymnasiums and computer rooms. It also helps to organize training sessions in Shanghai and Beijing for teachers from schools in backward areas. Project Hope has established a complete system for supporting students from poor families to attend primary and secondary schools and colleges in rural areas, and children of rural parents working in cities. By 2006, with a total of 3.2 billion yuan, Project Hope had supported over 2.9 million poor students, built 12,700 primary schools, established over 200 Web schools, donated 13,000 libraries, and trained more than 30,000 teachers for rural primary schools.

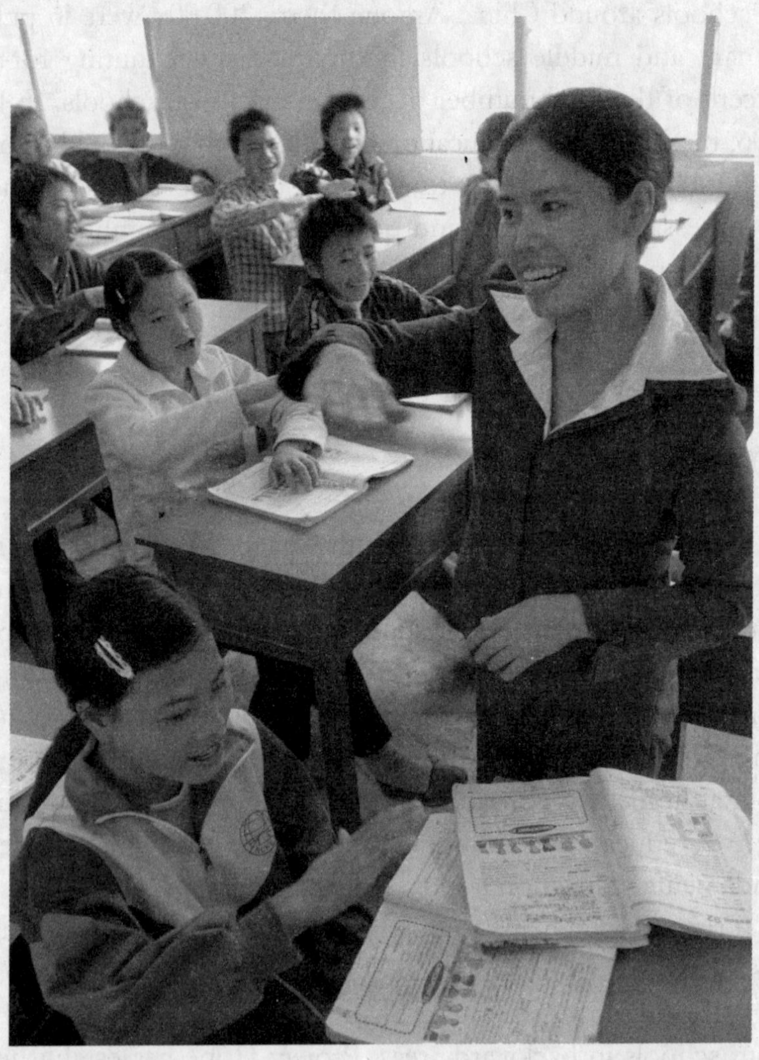

Jia Zhongqin, one of the first volunteers to go to China's western region, teaches an English class at the Daying Hope School, Ziyun County, Guizhou Province.

211工程
Project 211

Project 211 aims to give priority to the construction of some 100 institutions of higher learning and a number of key disciplinary areas. It is an important campaign of the Chinese government to develop and adapt higher education for China's economic and social development. The project was initiated in 1995 as a key State construction program and part of the mid- and long-term national economic and social development strategies. The State Council set up the Project 211 Coordination Group among ministries, composed of related directors of the State Council, the State Development and Reform Commission, the Ministry of Education and the Ministry of Finance. The Coordination Group makes decisions on major policies regarding the project.

The guiding principle of Project 211 is to let colleges and universities serve economic and social development. It concentrates on improving the capacity to transfer scientific research and education achievements into practical production by combining regional economic progress and social development. Many institutions of higher learning made the necessary reforms in terms of management, teaching, logistics and scientific research. They also adopted some new measures for innovation and talent fostering.

985工程
Project 985

In May, 1998, President Jiang Zemin, also the general-secretary of the CPC, declared at the celebrations for the

100th anniversary of Peking University: "China must have a number of first-grade universities of the international advanced level in the process of its modernization." Thereupon, the Ministry of Education announced the "Rejuvenation Program for Education in the 21st Century." This is Project 985 (The number refers to the month and year when the project began). The Ministry signed cooperative agreements with appropriate provincial and municipal governments in 1999 to upgrade dozens of leading higher-learning institutions to the advanced international level in the first two decades of the 21st century.

扩招

Enlargement of Recruitment of Higher Education

China's higher education includes general higher education and adult higher education. General higher education is divided into three phases: vocational training courses (two to three years), undergraduate courses (four to five years) and postgraduate courses (including master and doctorate courses). Aiming at becoming an internationally-acclaimed country of popular higher learning, China began enlarging its recruitment of students for higher education in 1999. In 2003, the number of students enrolled in colleges and universities had increased to 3.82 million from 1.6 million in 1999.

In 2006, in accordance with the spirit of "focusing on the quality of education and controlling the increase of recruitment to thoroughly apply the scientific outlook on development," the number of students in various higher learning institutions reached 25 million in 2006, an increase of only one percent over the previous year. In the same year, the general and adult higher learning institutions and higher vocational schools nationwide recruited 7.24 million students. Among them, 5.4 million entered general higher learning institutions and higher vocational schools, a seven-percent increase over the previous year but a 10.8 percent drop compared to the average during the Tenth Five-Year Plan period (2001-2005). In addition, 398,000 postgraduates were recruited, a 9.1 percent increase over the previous year but 2.7 percentage points lower than the growth rate in the same period in 2005.

国家助学贷款

State Student Loan Policy

The State student loan policy is jointly organized by banks and the State education administration. It enables children from families with financial difficulties to attend college or receive vocational education. The students apply for interest-free loans through colleges to cover some of their tuition, accommodation, and cost of living. They pay back the loans in installments after graduation. The maximum for each student is 6,000 yuan per academic year. The policy started in 1999, and had provided 2.465 million students nationwide with a total of 23.85 billion yuan by the end of October 2007.

At the same time, China also provides scholarships worth 8,000 yuan each every year to 50,000 outstanding students attending general higher learning institutions and full-time higher vocational schools. State scholarships for outstanding students from families with financial difficulties in general higher learning institutions and full-time higher vocational schools are worth 5,000 yuan each per year, and the students granted this scholarship account for, on average, three percent of all students in institutions of higher learning. In addition, the central and local governments have set up State Stipends for students from families with financial difficulties who are attending general higher learning institutions, full-time higher vocational schools and secondary vocational schools. On average, about 20 percent of students in general higher learning institutions and full-time higher vocational schools receive this stipend, worth 2,000 yuan a year. The stipend for students in secondary vocational schools is 1,500 yuan per person each year for the first two years. In the third year the student will take part in a work-study program and work as an intern.

高考经济
UEE Economy

The University Entrance Examination (UEE) economy heats up when the UEE comes round every year. Tonics purportedly for strengthening the brain and memory are hawked, and all kinds of examination aids fill the bookstores. Hotels have special rooms for examinees, and restaurants offer them special menus. Websites have "experts answer" programs and "chats with top examinees" programs. Even housekeeping companies provide special "UEE nurses."

Moreover, there is also the so-called "post-UEE economy," business offering preferential prices for examinees after the UEE and before the university term begins. Stores give rebates or return presents to examinees upon presentation of a UEE certificate. Restaurants recommend "thanking teacher banquets," tourist agencies offer "special trips for deepening understanding of knowledge," and beauty parlors offer lower prices to UEE students.

高考移民

UEE Migrants

Some examinees transfer their household registration to another province (autonomous region or municipality directly under the central government) where the university entrance standards are lower, therefore increasing their chances of being admitted into universities. They are called "UEE migrants." Most of these UEE migrants move to the areas where universities are concentrated (like Beijing, Shanghai) and the areas with favorable policy (like Hainan, Xinjiang, Qinghai) that have an apparently lower UEE mark lines.

大学生志愿服务西部计划

"Go West" Graduate Volunteer Program

This program was launched in June 2003, sending college graduates every year to village- or township-level administrations in western China for one or two years' service on a voluntary basis. In 2006, 6,253 were selected from among the 55,347 graduates who signed up for the program. Including the two-year term volunteers recruited in 2005, there were over 10,000 altogether.

The scope of services of the program is constantly being extended, and now covers ten fields—teaching, medical care, agriculture, construction and management of youth centers, distance education of cadres in rural areas, rural cultural development, grass-roots courts, grass-roots procuratorates, grass-roots law assistance and finance.

A graduate of Anshan University of Science and Technology, Long Hui, volunteers in his spare time to give classes to the Dickey Orphanage in Lhasa, Tibet.

大学生就业
Employment of College Graduates

When it comes to the employment of college graduates,

the Chinese government follows the principle featuring market orientation, government regulation, school recommendation and dual direction choices by students and employers. According to the survey titled, "The Employment Situation of College Graduates in 2006" carried out by the education department of the Chinese Communist Youth League, 41.6 percent of all college students believe that the most effective way to obtain a job is through the family's or personal social connections or recommendation by acquaintances. The salary expectation of 66.1 percent of students ranges from 1,000 yuan to 2,000 yuan per month. Graduates in agricultural subjects (not favored by many) have the highest rate of employment, and those from universities in eastern China also have a relatively higher employment rate than those from other parts of China.

A national human resources exchange center in Xicheng District, Beijing

From 1995 on, the central government began organizing examinations for the employment of college graduates as civil servants. In 2003, the number of people registered for the examination reached 360,000, and rose to one million in 2005, far more than the number of posts available. Job security, relatively high social status and gradually increasing welfare are among the reasons why so many college graduates want to become civil servants.

圆梦行动

Project for Realizing the College Dream

The "Project for Realizing the College Dream" is a public service project launched by the "Universal Focus" program of CCTV and the China Youth Development Foundation. Some 33 provincial youth development foundations and over 100 media organs are participants.

The project aims to mobilize social funds to help students from poor families "realize the college dream." The first year of the project saw 150 million yuan collected for 40,000 students who had passed the UEE but couldn't afford college tuition fees. The project has received great attention from State leaders, Communist Party committees at various levels, local governments and people of all walks of life. Premier Wen Jiabao greeted the "Universal Focus" crew personally, and Vice-premier Wu Yi raised US$ 200,000 for students from poor families in the Guangxi Zhuang Autonomous Region.

In 2007, the "Project for Realizing the College Dream" focused on students from poor rural families, to encourage the public to help the government in the solution to social problems, mainly through the media. The programs tell the stories of students from poor families striving for success. A total of 500 million people all over the country participated in the project in 2007, collecting more than 200 million yuan for 50,000 students.

科技

Science and Technology

创新型国家

Innovative Country

The Chinese government regards technological progress and innovation as the principal motive powers for boosting the national economy and social progress through enhancing self-innovation ability as the core link to readjust the economic structure, transform the growth mode and strengthen China's international competitive power.

At the moment, there are about 20 generally acknowledged innovative countries in the world, including the US, Japan, Finland and South Korea. The characteristics shared by these countries are: the composite innovation index exceeds those of other countries by far; the scientific progress contribution rate is over 70 percent; R&D expenditure generally accounts for two percent of GDP; and dependence on external technology is less than 30 percent. In addition, these countries have the highest rate of tripartite patents (warranted by USA, European countries and Japan). According to relevant research reports, due to its inferior innovative ability, China ranks 24th in a list of 48 major countries which account for 92 percent of the world's GDP. According to the *National Medium- and Long-Term Science and Technology Strategy (2006-2020)* promulgated by the State Council on February 9, 2006, China hopes to join the list of innovative countries by 2020.

创新型企业

Innovative Enterprises

The National Conference on Science and Technology, held in early 2006, and the *National Medium- and Long-Term Science and*

Technology Strategy (2006-2020), promulgated later, set the goal of establishing a national innovation system with Chinese characteristics through a technology innovation system created by integrating production, study and research, taking enterprises as the main body and with market needs as the guidance. The list of 103 innovative enterprises as experimental units collaboratively selected by the Ministry of Science and Technology, State-owned Assets Supervision and Administration Commission and All-China Federation of Trade Unions has been made public. It includes the China Netcom (Group) Company Ltd, Zhong Xing Telecommunication Equipment Co. Ltd, Huawei Technologies Co. Ltd, Datang Co. Ltd and other companies, which will obtain corresponding supports in policy, finance and other respects from the central government. The three ministries and commissions mentioned above came to an agreement in adding the number of experimental innovative enterprises to the number of 500 within three to five years. A batch of promising innovative enterprises, like Huawei Technologies Co. Ltd, ZTE Corporation, Haier Group, Lenovo Group, Chery Automobile Co. Ltd, Geely Holding Group, Huazhong Numerical Control Co. Ltd, Shen Hua Group Corporation Ltd and Shanghai Baosteel Group Corporation, have grown rapidly along with the development of China's economy since the reform and opening-up policies were introduced. Enterprises' enthusiasm for technical innovation has been enhanced with the further implementation of the reform of the science and technology and economic systems. The expenditures for research and development in Chinese enterprises reached 167.4 billion *yuan* in 2005, an increase of 42 percent compared with only 53.7 billion *yuan* in 2000. In 2000, Chinese enterprises owned only 28 percent of the patents for domestic service inventions within China, but this had risen to 52 percent by 2005.

There are few internationally competitive innovative enterprises in China. And this situation does not match the country's ranking of the world's sixth-largest economy. Only 19 mainland enterprises were listed in the top 500 selected by *Fortune* magazine in 2006, and most of them are monopoly or resource enterprises. China's inferior position in international trade and the system of global division of industries is directly related to the country's shortage of strong competitive innovative enterprises. Generally, weakness in technology innovation ability prevents Chinese enterprises from joining the main body of technology innovation. In 2005, the investment in R&D of medium- and large-sized enterprises was only 0.76 percent, and only 38.7 percent of the total number of enterprises carried out scientific and technological activities. Besides, only 23.7 percent of the enterprises had R&D units. Only three out of 10,000 domestic enterprises owned IPR (intellectual property rights) of core technologies, and 98.6 percent of enterprises had never applied for any patent.

神州五号

Shenzhou-V Spacecraft

Shenzhou-V, a China-made manned spacecraft, was launched successfully from the Jiuquan Satellite Launch Center on March 15, 2003, and landed safely with only a 4.8-km error from the theoretical impact spot in the Inner Mongolia Autonomous Region after orbiting the earth 14 times. The first Chinese astronaut, Yang Liwei, walked out of the unimpaired re-entry module by himself. This feat symbolized a breakthrough for China in manned space technology, and made the country the third in the world after Russia and the US to independently master manned space technology. Before this, China had successfully launched four experimental unmanned spacecraft: the first on November 20, 1999 (Shenzhou-I); the second on January 10, 2001 (Shenzhou-II); the third on March 25, 2002 (Shenzhou-III); and the fourth on December 30, 2002 (Shenzhou-IV).

In January 1991, the central government approved the manned space flight project, consisting of seven aspects — astronaut training, spacecraft applications, manned astronautic flight, carrier rockets, launch site, landing ground and spaceflight observation, and control and communications. This project was the largest in scale, most complicated in system and most difficult in technology in China's spaceflight history. China's manned spaceflight project was divided into three stages: The first was the launching of unmanned, and then manned, spacecraft to send the astronaut safely to the perigee orbit to conduct scientific experiments and observe the earth, and to guarantee that the astronaut would return safely; the second was allowing the astronaut to walk in space, complete docking between the spacecraft and capsule, launch a long-term automatic skylab under the short-term manned management, and establish complete set of space project systems as soon as possible; and the last was to establish a large-scale and long-term manned space station.

神州六号

Shenzhou-VI Spacecraft

Shenzhou-VI's successful launch from the Jiuquan Satellite Launch Center on October 12, 2005 marked a significant advance in China's manned spaceflight undertaking. After spending 115 hours and 32 minutes in perfect spaceflight, the re-entry

Fei Junlong and Nie Haisheng, the two astronauts who circled the earth in China's Shenzhou VI spaceship, exercise in the recovery capsule.

module of Shenzhou-VI returned and landed successfully, and two astronauts Fei Junlong and Nie Haisheng walked out of the module safely at 4:33 am on October 17, 2005.

Shenzhou-VI made many first steps in several scientific domains for China's spaceflight industry, such as more than one astronaut engaged in experimental spaceflight for several days to lay the foundation for working and living in space in the future; the astronauts entered and shuttled the orbit module to carry out experiments involving the closing of the door of the re-entry module and checking for leaks in a state of weightlessness; they conducted the first manned space science experiments in the fields of bioscience and materials science, earth survey, ocean pollution monitoring, atmospheric layer survey and vegetation survey; they tried several innovations in space life, such as putting on and off pressure suits, tasting hot meals and reconstituted foods, used a "space closestool," drank mineral water from 1,700 m under the ground, measured their blood pressure, slept in sleeping bags and took the first photos of on-orbit anti-disturbance experiments.

神州七号

Shenzhou-VII Spacecraft

Planned for launching in 2008, Shenzhou-VII, the seventh spacecraft in the Shenzhou series, will carry three astronauts who will make China's first space walk and complete the spacecraft docking.

After Shenzhou-VII's launch, China will establish a short-term skylab for astronauts and a long-term experimental space station as the preliminary provisions for the final establishment of China's own space station.

探月工程

The Lunar Exploration Project

As early as in 1994 Chinese space scientists began to research the possibility of lunar exploration. In 1996 they had completed the technical program of the lunar exploration satellite, solved the key technology problems by 1998 and put together the three-stage plan of "Orbiting," "Landing" and "Returning" in 2004.

The launch of the "Chang'E-I" lunar satellite was the first phase of the project for probing the surface environment, geomorphological structure, terrain, geological structure and physical field of the moon. The project plan for the second phase has been accomplished, and the stage of technology breakthrough is near. The second phase is expected to be accomplished by 2013, when a landing probe will also be launched.

The "Returning" part of the plan is scheduled to be accomplished in 2017. In the meantime, the relevant departments are researching deep space probe possibilities in the future, including a landing on the Mars and other minor planets.

At 18:05 on October 24, 2007, China's first lunar module "Chang'E-I" was launched successfully from the Xichang Satellite Launch Center, symbolizing a new breakthrough in the development and research of China's satellite technology. There were 12 technological innovations in the "Chang'E-I" satellite — general optimization design, track design, guidance, navigation and control, heat-control design, long-distance tracking telemetering & control system, large-angle mechanical scanning directive aerial, complete satellite self-management, actual load, power supply, drive, structure design, and integration testing design. There were 44 innovation points in the complete satellite and its sub-systems. By the end of 2007, 20 patents concerning the satellite and its sub-systems were pending, and 37 other patents had been applied for.

Ye Peijian, an academician of the Chinese Academy of Sciences and the chief designer of the "Chang'E-I" satellite, said that the satellite ranks among the world's leaders in its field.

国家科学技术奖

National Science and Technology Awards

The Chinese government promulgated the *Provisional Regulations on Bonuses Awarded by the Chinese Academy of Sciences* as early as 1955, aiming at rewarding people who made significant scientific and technological achievements. In 1984 the National Awards for Scientific and Technological Progress were established. The Top State Award for Science and Technology was established in May 1999, and is bestowed annually by the president of the People's Republic of China at the National Conference on Science and Technology. There are altogether five national science and technology awards — for progress in science and technology, natural sciences, technological inventions, scientific and technological progress, and international cooperation in science and technology.

In February 2007 Li Zhensheng, an academician of the Chinese Academy of Sciences, geneticist and expert on wheat breeding, was the winner of the 2006 Top State Science and Technology Award. At the same time, 29 natural sciences awards, 56 technical invention awards and 241 scientific and technological progress awards were given out. So far, nine scientists had won the Top State Science and Technology Award.

国家科技攻关计划

National Key Science and Technology Project

As China's largest scientific and technological project of the 20th century since the reform and opening-up policies were introduced, the National Key Science and Technology Project was approved by the Fifth Session of the Fifth National People's Congress on November 30, 1982. The project's goal is to solve instructional, decisive and comprehensive problems connected with agriculture, electronic information, energy resources, transportation, materials, resources survey, environment protection, medical treatment and sanitation, etc, which have been present in the development of society and the national economy for a long time. With the largest investment and the most manpower, it is, so far, the largest science and technology undertaking with the biggest influence on the national economy.

The implementation of the National Key Science and Technology Project has played a significant role in the sustainable development of China's economy, science and technology, national defense and society. During the period of the Tenth Five-Year Plan (2001-2005), the Project arranged 210 important and significant items in the eight fields of agriculture, information, automation, materials, resources and transportation, source and environment, medical treatment and sanitation, and public services. And during the period of the 11th Five-year Plan (2006-2010) the Project, stressing development and research of public service technology, core general technologies, enterprise participation and the mechanism of the combination of manufacturing, study and research, will strongly back up industries in the fields of energy resources, natural resources, environment, agriculture, medicine and sanitation.

863 计划
The National 863 Program

In March 1986, the National High Technology Research and Development Program of China (also known as the 863 Program), referring to 15 topics of seven high-technology domains, was initiated after comprehensive evaluation by hundreds of Chinese scientists. In 1993, communications technology was listed in the 863 Program as a major component. From 1991 to 1995, the State Science and Technology Commission included rice genome technology, an airborne remote sensing image real-time transmitting system, the core technology of the HJD-04 large programmed digital switcher and superconducting technology as special items in the Program. In July 1996, ocean resources exploitation technology was made the eighth domain in the Program after approval by a panel of the State Science and Technology Commission. Now the Program includes 20 topics of eight domains — biotechnology, space technology, information technology, laser technology, automation technology, energy technology, advanced materials technology and marine technology.

In the implementation of the Program, government departments conduct macro-adjustment and control and services, while scientists take charges of the general research direction and relevant specific items. The responsibilities of the Program's team of expert include closely following the latest trends in the world's advanced science and technology, submit annual research reports concerning their own domains and identify new research trends. In addition, rapid application of new findings to industry is a prominent characteristic of the Program.

973 计划
The 973 Program

Beginning in 1998, the National Key Basic Research Program (also known as the 973 Program) was set up to conduct overall research in the domains of agriculture, energy resources, information, natural resources and the environment, population and health, and materials, to offer scientific and theoretical references for solving relevant problems. The Program encourages leading scientists to carry out basic research in frontier sciences and advanced technologies.

Collaborating with the National Natural Science Foundation

of China and other related departments, the Ministry of Science and Technology, which has the principal responsibility for the whole Project, has adopted the "2+3" mode, which evaluates the efficiency and potential of the research items in the first two years, and then sets the overall research plan for the following three years. From 1998 to 2002, the Program embarked on 132 items — 17 in agriculture, 15 in energy resources, 17 in information technology, 24 in resources and the environment, 21 in population and health, 19 in materials and 19 in important frontier sciences.

火炬计划

The Torch Program

Under the instructions of the Ministry of Science and Technology (the former State Science and Technology Commission), the Torch Program was made the guiding program for China's new and high-tech industries by the Chinese government in August 1988. As China's most important high-tech industry program, it shoulders the responsibility of realizing the commercialization, industrialization and globalization of scientific achievements as its own goals, including organizing a batch of high-tech development items with advanced technologies, excellent domestic and overseas markets and high profits, establishing a batch of high-tech-industry development zones and seeking an efficient administration system and operation mechanism for high-tech industries. The important items cover advanced materials technology, biotechnology, electronic information technology, electromechanical integration technology, new resources technology, energy-saving technology and other advanced technologies.

Since 1996, the Chinese government has taken some corresponding steps annually including certifying a batch of significant items from the Torch Program for aid; in collaboration with local governments, selecting a batch of potential high-tech enterprises (groups) from those engaged in the Program to offer abundant support in terms of markets, information, capital, management and services to help the development of local economies; establishing the Software Industry Base of the National Torch Program to promote the applicability of software research and foster small- and medium-sized software enterprises.

星火计划

The Spark Program

The name of this program originated in Chairman Mao's saying that "a single spark can start a prairie fire," which was quoted by the State Science and Technology Commission when it proposed to the State Council boosting the development of the local economy through fostering a batch of scientific projects of "little investment, short duration but quick returns" in May 1985. The "Spark Program" meant that the spark of science and technology would spread prosperity over all the rural areas of China. The Program was finally approved by the central government in early 1986, with the aim of boosting the rural economy through the progress of science and technology, popularizing scientific technologies in rural areas and leading rural residents to a better-off life.

The principal contents of the Program consist of supporting advanced technical projects with little investment but quick returns, and making full use of rural resources; establishing science and technology enterprises in the rural areas and setting up demonstrations of the structural adjustment of rural industries and products; researching and developing batch-produced equipment applied to rural enterprises; training a batch of rural technical and administrative personnel, and peasant entrepreneurs; developing high-yield, high-quality and high-efficiency agriculture to fuel the construction of socialized services in the rural areas and the development of rural economies of scale; and establishing Spark Technology-Intensive Zones with science and technology leading the way for regional pillar industries. So far, the Program has implemented over 150,000 scientific and technological demonstration projects covering more than 90 percent of the rural areas of the country.

748 计划
Project 748

In August 1974, with the approval of Premier Zhou Enlai, an important scientific research project — the Chinese Character Information Processing System, also known as the "748 Project," was put into operation. It consists of three sub-projects: Chinese Character Communication, Chinese Character Information Retrieval and Precise Filmsetting of Chinese Characters. Initiating the second technical revolution in China's printing industry, the Project led the way to adapting Chinese characters to the era of computers and lasers.

In 1975, Wang Xuan of Beijing University came up with a plan to research and develop the precise phototypesetting of Chinese characters — the fourth-generation laser phototypesetting system. In 1986, the new Chinese character laser phototypesetting system was appraised as one of China's top ten technical achievements and won a gold medal at the Geneva International Inventions Exhibition. In 1987, the system was awarded the top National Scientific and Technological Progress Award, and Wang Xuan also became the winner of the first Bi Sheng Award. In May 1987, the *Economic Daily* became the first Chinese newspaper to use computer to do the page composition, and output whole page film by laser phototypesetting technology. By 1993, nearly 99 percent of newspaper offices and 95 percent book and periodical printers had been equipped with the China-made computerized laser phototypesetting system. This printing revolution bade farewell to the old hot metal printing system, and welcomed the era of laser and cyber culture.

2049 计划

Program 2049

Aiming at improving scientific knowledge among all the Chinese people, in 1999 the China Association for Science and Technology proposed the "Program 2049" to the Chinese government. The plan envisages equipping the Chinese people with the scientific knowledge they need to develop their society and economy to the levels of those of a moderately developed country by 2049, the year of the 100th anniversary of the founding of the People's Republic of China. Formally launched in October 2003, the Program, as part of the national drive for quality-oriented education, utilizes the functions of all kinds of out-of-school activities venues, including science and technology museums, to cooperate with educational and teaching reforms, and develop talented people for the country.

According to *The Outline of the Action Plan for Improving the Scientific Quality of All the People (2006-2010-2020)* promulgated in March 2006, by 2010, we should reach the level of the developed countries of the late 1980s through scientific education, transmission and popularization, and improvements in the citizens' qualities; by 2020, depending on the rapid development of the items mentioned above, we should establish complete sets of organizational practices, basic constructions, guaranteed conditions, supervision and evaluation, etc., to ensure a striking advance in the level of the scientific knowledge of all the people, and reach the level of the developed countries in the early 21st century.

百千万人才工程

The New Century National Project of Hundred, Thousand and Ten Thousand Talents

In 1995, cooperating with related departments, the Ministry of Personnel of the People's Republic of China put forward the "New Century National Project of Hundred, Thousand and Ten Thousand Talents," aiming at fostering more young academic forerunners. By 2000, the number of nominees in all fields had reached nearly 10,000, and a complete system for developing young and excellent talented people of all kinds through multi-channels had been established. In 2002, the Ministry of Personnel completed the work plan of the 2002-2010 New Century Project of Hundred, Thousand and Ten Thousand Talents.

The goals of the Project are: first, by 2010, to have trained hundreds of excellent world-class scientists, engineering experts and theorists; second, thousands of domestic forerunners with advanced levels in scientific and technological fields; and third, tens of thousands of potential young talents with great influence in all relevant fields. The nominees in the first two categories will be selected by the central government once every two years with a total number of about 500, while those in the third category will be selected by provincial governments. Besides, the top 100 out of the 500 state-class nominees will be appraised and selected in relevant disciplines which possess clear innovative goals to fuel the development of the frontier sciences and raise China's status in the world's science and technology fields; and the other 400 will be regarded as a reserve of high-class and much-needed skills in vital fields connected with the development of society and the national economy. The related departments of all provinces and autonomous regions should take charge of the selection and cultivation of provincial and ministerial talented people.

中关村电脑节

Zhongguancun Computer Festival

Zhongguancun, the "Silicon Valley of China," represents China's most advanced computer technology level with the largest-scale market, the most computer manufacturers and the best-equipped electronic facilities.

After more than 20 years' development, Zhongguancun has become the leader in the information technology industries not only in Beijing but also in the whole country. The Zhongguancun Computer Festival has been held annually for a number of years. Jointly sponsored by the Administration Committee of the Beijing New Technology Industry Development and Experimental Zone and the government of Haidian District, and undertaken by the administration committee of the Haidian Scientific Experimental Zone, the first Zhongguancun Computer Festival was held May 8-12, 1998. The festival comprised

Subject Seminar, Display of Top-notch Software, Computer Demonstration and Popularization, Discount Sales, Laws and Regulations Dissemination and Consultation, Exhibition of Leading Electronic Publications, Talks on Scientific and Technological Projects, Experience Exchanges, and the launch of polls like the "Information Rapido," and the Top Ten Computer Brands.

Zhongguancun, known as China's "Silicon Valley," is a high-tech industrial area. The Zhongguancun Computer Festival is held here every year. The picture shows the Zhongguancun Square.

文化

Culture

双百方针

The Guidelines of "Letting a Hundred Flowers Blossom and Letting a Hundred Schools of Thought Contend"

These guidelines were put forward by Chairman Mao Zedong on April 28, 1956 at an enlarged meeting of the Political Bureau of the CPC Central Committee: " 'Letting a hundred flowers blossom and letting a hundred schools of thought contend,' I think, should become our guidelines. As for art, we should let a hundred flowers blossom; as for academic learning, we should let a hundred schools of thought contend." Since then, these guidelines have become the basic ones for advancing China's art and science as well as bringing prosperity to its socialist culture.

The content of the guidelines is the practice of socialist democracy in academic circles, allowing different forms and genres of art to contend freely; to let different schools coexist; and to resolve what is right or wrong in the academic and literary fields by means of free discussion, academic research and practice, instead of through administrative mandates.

新闻联播

CCTV News

CCTV News is a 30-minute news program broadcast over Channel One of China Central Television (CCTV) every day at 19:00 Beijing time, reporting news of China and the world, as well as of sports. The news is repeated at 21:00 through the news channel and at 01:00 through CCTV International. It is also broadcast simultaneously by the main channels of local TV stations. CCTV News is regarded as authoritative and influential, and has the highest television viewing rating.

CCTV News, launched on January 1, 1978, broadcasts live from 19:00 to 19:20 every day. On September 1, 1982, China shifted its major news release from 20:00 to 19:00 via the CCTV News program, marking the debut of CCTV as an official news agency in its own right.

金鸡百花奖
Golden Rooster Awards

The Golden Rooster Awards are China's top film prizes. The awards have been given annually by the China Film Association since 1981 (the Year of the Rooster) to honor excellent films and outstanding film workers. Using a golden rooster to symbolize fair and free competition, the awards are also an encouragement to film workers to improve their products. The highest honor for film workers in China's mainland, the award winners are appraised and selected by film professionals, and are bestowed every May 23 at a grand ceremony. The Hundred Flowers Awards, founded in 1962 at the proposal of Premier Zhou Enlai, are evaluated and chosen by the general public. Since the founding of the Golden Rooster Awards in 1981, these two awards have been combined into the Golden Rooster and Hundred Flowers Awards. The awards ceremony, which became a film festival, started at the First Golden Rooster and Hundred Flowers Film Festival in 1992.

The festival is held annually at different places, helping to promote cinematographic art, publicize domestic films, and boost the close relationship between film workers and the public. The Golden Rooster and Hundred Flowers Film Festival has become a national grand cultural activity combining film appraisal, awards ceremony, showing of new domestic and overseas films, seminars, film market, international cultural exchanges and literary performances.

第五代百花奖

Fifth-generation Directors

The fifth-generation directors mainly refer to those who graduated from the Beijing Film Academy in the 1980s. They have an acute sense of new ideas and film techniques, desiring to explore the history of Chinese culture and the psychological structure of the Chinese nation. Their works are subjective, symbolic and allegorical. This generation is mainly represented by such directors as Chen Kaige, Zhang Yimou and Feng Xiaogang. The year 1988 saw Feng's "Red Sorghum" win the Golden Bear Award at the Berlin International Film Festival. It was the first time for a Chinese film maker to ascend the prize-winning stage at one of the three largest world film festivals (Berlin, Venice and Cannes). Subsequent years continues to witness Chinese film workers prominent at the major international film festivals. Chen's "Farewell My Concubine" and Zhang's "Ju Dou" and "Raise the Red Lantern" earned Oscar nominations for the Best Foreign-language Movie.

In the new market economy system, the fifth generation of Chinese film directors has embarked on large-scale film production. They have accepted international rules, and are beginning to aim at the international market, catering to foreign tastes and stressing film commercialization. However, China's popular films are attempting to align with international standards while displaying excessively Chinese elements, making it difficult to deal with their merits and demerits.

上海国际电影节

Shanghai International Film Festival

The Shanghai International Film Festival, co-hosted by the State Administration of Radio, Film and Television and the Shanghai Municipal Government, is China's sole internationally A-rated feature film festival. It is recognized as one of the world's nine major international film festivals. The birthplace of Chinese cinema, Shanghai, holds the nine-day film festival every June. Since 1993, the festival has attracted hundreds of domestic and overseas films for exhibition and competition.

The Shanghai International Film Festival consists of four major activities: film appraisal and selection for the Jin Jue Award, international film exhibition, international film transactions, and seminars on international films. The Jin Jue Award in eight categories is evaluated by an international appraisal committee. To encourage Asian film creation by new directors and introduce Asian films to the rest of the world, the Shanghai International Film Festival established an Asian New Talent Award in 2004.

数字电视

Digital Television

Owing to its interactive, simulative and low-distortion features, digital television has much better audio and visual functions than traditional television. The standard for China's digital-terrestrial-television broadcasting system took effect on August 1, 2007. China has a tremendous market for digital television. It is estimated that China's digital television users will increase from over one million in 2004 to over 40 million in 2009. At present, China has about 115 million cable television subscribers. If they all turned to digital television, a market of 300 billion yuan-worth would be created in the digital television industry, including set-top boxes and television sets.

The State Administration of Radio, Film and Television launched live digital satellite television service in 2006, and will promote its terrestrial digital television service in 2008. Analog television service will be ended in 2015.

青歌大赛

Young Vocalist Competition

The Young Vocalist Competition is hosted by China Central Television (CCTV) and coordinated by local provincial television stations. It is an important venue for introducing new vocalists. Beginning in 1984, the competition is held every two years.

In the second competition the participants were grouped into amateurs and professionals, and the performances into bell canto, Chinese traditional songs and popular songs. In the eighth competition, teamwork and overall quality evaluation were added to the judges' criteria. A supervising team was added at the ninth competition to improve the level of fairness of the judging. A new generation of musicians and singers joined the appraisal committee, and the favorite singer award was chosen by audience votes. The tenth competition saw great successes achieved by ethnic-minority singers. The 12th competition allowed amateurs and professionals to form combined teams.

Other competitions which give young vocalists a chance to present themselves to the Chinese public are CCTV Channel Two's *China Dream*, Hunan Satellite TV's *Super Voice Girls* and Shanghai Oriental Satellite TV's *My Shape, My Show*.

超女

Super Girl

Super Girl, abbreviated from Super Voice Girls, is an entertainment program broadcast by Hunan TV Satellite to foster musical talents. Any female above the age of 16 who loves singing, from any part of China, may submit an application to appear on the show. The winner is chosen by audience vote.

The show was an instant success nationwide when it was first broadcast in 2005. Three top participants in Super Girl have become popular idols.

At the first stage, the show imitated Britain's Pop Idol television talent contest, in which the competitors sing songs chosen by themselves without musical accompaniment. The appraisal committee, usually two men and one woman, is composed of senior people in musical circles. They can interrupt anytime with ironical comments. At the second stage, 50 competitors go through several elimination rounds in different regions, and come out the regional champions. This is followed by the final national contest to choose the top three. At the first Super Girl show in 2004, the top three in the final were An Youqi, Wang Ti and Zhang Hanyun. At the second, in 2005, Li Yuchun, Zhou Bichang and Zhang Liangying took championship, runner-up and third places, respectively in the Super Girl final, and at the third, in 2006, the top three were Shang Wenjie, Tan Weiwei and Liu Liyang.

网络红人

Online Favorites

Also known as online celebrities, online favorites are figures who were or are popular on the Internet. The birth of online celebrities is no different from that of film or TV stars. They are the inevitable outcome of the powerful discourses via the Internet — the new arising media. The differences between online favorites and traditional ones are the platform they exist.

Generally speaking, the online favorites are divided into three kinds: first, those in the age of text; second, those in the age of text and picture; third, those in the age of broadband access. The first kind includes Pizicai, Ningcaishen, Li Xunhuan, Annibaobei. In the time of the Internet with a band width of 56 k or earlier, the text creates online favorites, which share a common feature of living by the text.

After the Internet enters the age of text and pictures, the favorites start to be as colorful as fashion magazines. In this age, more online female favorites appear, such as Furong Jiejie (Sister Furong), Tianxian Meimei (Sister Tianxian), Eryue Yatou (February Girl) as well as the subsequent Wangluo Xiaopang (Internet Fatty). They all enjoy the advantage of presenting pictures on the Internet.

As the Internet gets a wider band width, entering the age of broadband, such figures as Hu Ge appear, followed by Houshe Nansheng (Back Dormitory Boys). The popularity of online songs by people such as Xiangxiang and Daolang are good signs for the online favorites in the age of broadband.

原生态

Original Folk Song

In recent years, original [folk song], a word borrowed from natural science, has become a buzz word to describe down-to-earth songs in folk music circles. It refers to a pure and unrefined song, which is not influenced much by the outside, formed during people's lives and work, circulating in certain regions, and passed on via oral tradition. China has a long history of folk songs developed in different regions. A large number of ethnic groups and their languages with their unique folk customs have fostered a rich tapestry of folk art. In the 1980s, China's traditional arts were collected in ten categories, among which the number of folk songs amounted to as many as 400,000. In 2004, China Central Television (CCTV) held its first western folk song competition, with the participation of more than 300 singers from over 30 ethnic groups. At the opening ceremony of the Nanning International Folk Song Festival, original folk songs became a focus of attention again. It became a new cultural focus in activities such as China's North-South Folk Song Competition and the ethnic folk song and dance "Yunnan Image," and a new highlight in the 2006 Young Vocalists Competition.

文化创意产业

Cultural and Creative Industry

In 2005, Beijing proposed to develop a cultural and creative industry, aiming to build a cultural and creative metropolis with international influence. In the light of the Investor's Guide to

The 798 Art Zone near Qiuxianqiao is Beijing's representative spot of the cultural creation industry.

Beijing's Cultural and Creative Industry, the city would put major emphases on eight categories — artistic performances, publishing, distribution and copyright, film and TV program production and trade, research and development of animated cartoons and online games, artifact business, design creativity, and cultural tours. In addition, it will loosen market access to this industry, and absorb overseas funds and social capital to develop it.

In 2005, Beijing's per capita GDP reached US$5,457, reflecting a great improvement in people's lives. Cultural consumption has become a new focus for residents. In light of the present annual rate of 15.1 percent growth for Beijing's cultural industry, the added value in this industry will have exceeded 100 billion yuan by 2010, making up over 10 percent of the city's total production value. Thus, it will become one of the pillar industries of the city's economy. Nowadays Beijing has a number of concentrated areas for cultural and creative industry, including 798 Art Zones, three animated cartoon bases, Panjiayuan Artifacts Market, and Happy Valley Amusement Park. Moreover, Beijing is planning to build a Chinese film and TV play production base, a high-tech park in the Zhongguancun area, a distribution center for printed materials, and a new international conference and exhibition center. In December 2006, Beijing held the first Beijing International Cultural and Creative Industry Expo. The Expo brought into full play Beijing's advantages, offering an international platform for cooperation in this industry.

中国结

Chinese Knots

Chinese knots are unique folk decorations. Over thousands of years, they have evolved into a refined handicraft popular among the public.

Chinese knots are tied using a single thread. Each Chinese knot has its own structure, and is named in accordance with its shape and significance. Chinese knots reflect ancient Chinese cultural beliefs and the people's yearning for truth, goodness and beauty. Attaching a *panchang* knot to a hook on a wedding occasion symbolizes a couple loving each other for ever. Decorating a jade pendant with a *ruyi* knot conveys the meaning of feeling gratified and having good luck in everything. Attaching a *jixiang* knot to a fan symbolizes auspiciousness, luck and goodliness. Mixing different types of knots with other auspicious ornaments constitutes a unique, colorful and connotative tradition among Chinese ornaments. Different combinations express good wishes as well as reverence.

Chinese Knots

世界文化和自然遗产
World Cultural and Natural Heritage

To protect the world cultural and natural heritage, the United Nations Educational, Scientific and Cultural Organization (UNESCO) approved at its 17th session the Convention for the Protection of the World Cultural and Natural Heritage on November 16, 1972. In 1976, the World Heritage Committee was founded, which draws up the World Heritage List. China joined the Convention on December 12, 1985, and became a member of the Committee on October 29, 1999.

The World Heritage body is made up of the World Cultural

Heritage (including places of cultural interest), the World Natural Heritage, and the World Cultural and Natural Heritage organizations. By July 2005 there were 812 world heritage sites, distributed in 137 countries. In 1987, China's Great Wall, the Forbidden City, Peking Man Site at Zhoukoudian, Mogao Caves of Dunhuang, Qin Shihuang Mausoleum and Terracotta Warriors, and Mount Taishan were included on the World Heritage List. During the 30th Congress of the World Heritage Committee in July 2006, China's Sichuan Giant Panda Sanctuaries and Yin Ruins in Anyang of Henan were added. By June 2007, 35 sites in China have been listed, ranking third in number behind Italy and Spain.

The terra-cotta warriors of the Qin Dynasty (221-206 BC) are part of China's world heritage treasures.

世界记忆工程

Memory of the World Program

The Memory of the World Program was launched in 1992 by the United Nations Educational, Scientific and Cultural Organization (UNESCO). Its mission is to protect and preserve the cultural heritage of the world under UNESCO's charter, promote the use of cultural heritage, and enhance the consciousness of the importance of the cultural heritage and its preservation. The Program concentrates on historical records, including manuscripts, valuable documents of any medium in libraries and archives, and oral historical records.

The Memory of the World Register collects such archives. So far, China has four documents included in the Memory of the World Register — the Chinese traditional music sound archive in the library of the graduate school of the China Academy of Art, the list of successful imperial examination candidates of the Qing Dynasty (1644-1911), the records of the grand secretariat of the Qing court and the Naxi Dongba manuscripts and imperial examination records in the Dongba Culture Institute of the Yunnan Provincial Academy of Social Sciences.

非物质文化遗产

Intangible Cultural Heritage

China's cultural heritage includes tangible and intangible treasures. The tangible cultural heritage covers artifacts of historical, artistic and scientific value. They include immovable cultural relics, including tombs, buildings, cave temples, stone inscriptions, frescoes, contemporary and modern historical sites and representative buildings, and movable cultural relics, including material objects, artworks, manuscripts and books. Also included are historical and cultural cities (districts and towns) that are unique in architectural style or location. The intangible cultural heritage refers to traditional cultural forms closely related to people's lives, and passed down through generations. It includes oral tradition, traditional performing arts, folk culture activities, traditional folk knowledge and practices relating to nature and the universe and traditional handicraft skills.

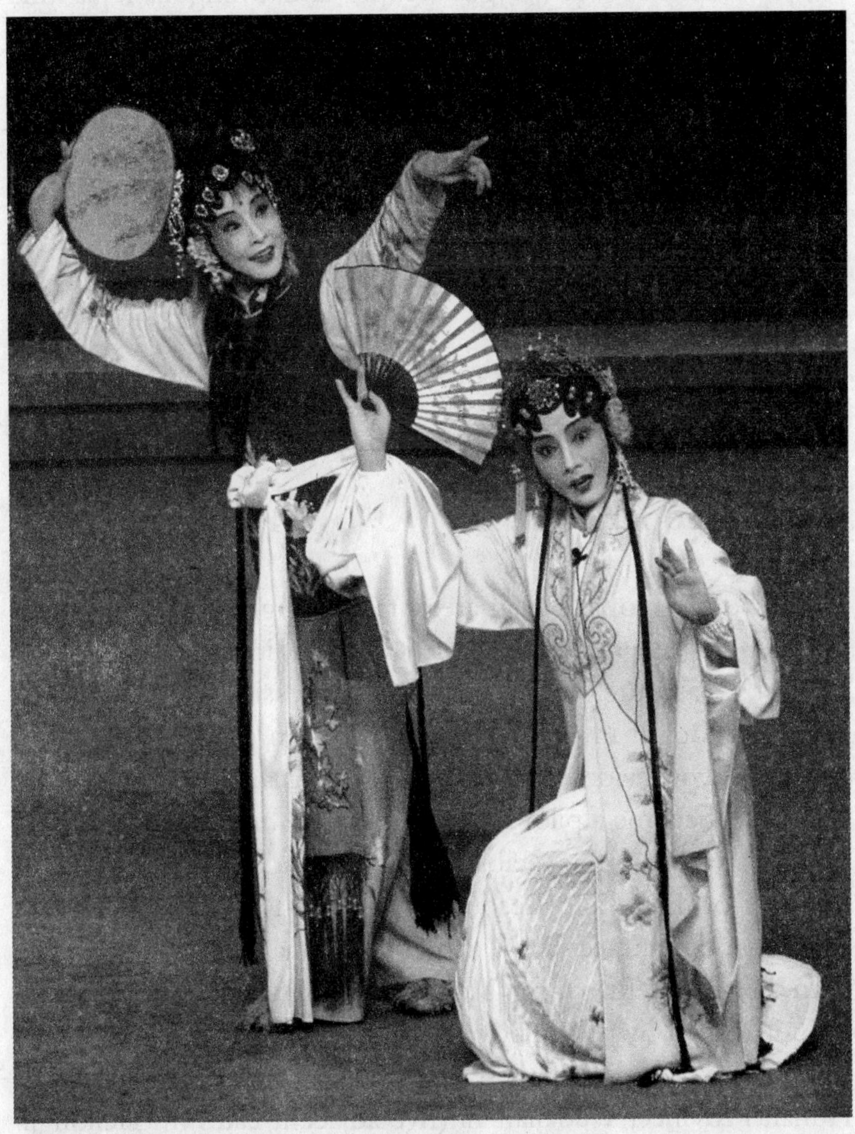

Kunqu opera, one of the world's intangible cultural heritages. The picture shows a scene from the Kunqu opera *Peony Pavilion*.

In 2000, UNESCO launched the Masterpieces of the Oral and Intangible Heritage of Humanity program. China's *kunqu* opera, the art of playing the *guqin* (seven-stringed zither), the Muqam music of the Uygur people and Mongolian pastoral songs were included in the program. Mongolian pastoral songs were submitted to the program in 2005 jointly by China and Mongolia, the first instance of such cooperation with UNESCO. In June 2006, China issued its first national intangible heritage list, containing 518 items, of which 150 are connected with the country's minority nationalities. The list also includes religion-related items, such as Daoist music, Buddhist music and exorcism dances.

世界地质公园

World Geopark

A World Geopark is an area of special geological and natural interest recognized by UNESCO. The idea of establishing geoparks was put forward at the 156th session of UNESCO's Executive Board in April 1999. Its mission is to establish 500 geoparks worldwide, with 20 geoparks to be set up annually. China has become a pilot country in establishing geoparks.

To coordinate the establishment of world geoparks, China's Ministry of Land and Resources set up an office and relevant evaluation committee. By March 2008, China had Mount Huangshan in Anhui Province, Mount Lushan in Jiangxi Province, Mount Yuntai in Henan Province, the Stone Forest in Yunnan Province, Mount Danxia in Guangdong Province, Zhangjiajie in Hunan Province, Wudalianchi (five adjacent lakes) in Heilongjiang Province, Mount Songshan in Henan Province, and other 12 geoparks.

文化遗产日

Cultural Heritage Day

In December 2005, the State Council issued the Recommendation for Strengthening Cultural Heritage Protection, setting the second Saturday of June each year as China's Cultural Heritage Day. China celebrated its first Cultural Heritage Day on June 10, 2006, with the theme of "Protecting the Cultural Heritage and Spiritual Garden."

In 1982, China promulgated the Law on Protecting Cultural Relics, which was revised again in 2002. By May 2006, there were 2,352 key national units in China for the protection of cultural relics, 9,396 provincial units, and 58,300 units in cities and counties. Moreover, there are another 103 historical and cultural cities. The central government increased the funds earmarked for cultural relic protection from 129 million yuan in 1994 to 534 million yuan in 2005. In 2003 China initiated the Folk Culture Protection Project to carry out the relevant work. In December 2005, the Ministry of Culture promulgated the Management Methods for Museums. The Law for the Protection of the Intangible Cultural Heritage was included in the 2007 plan for the National People's Congress. By 2006, China had over 2,300 museums of various kinds, and over 20 million special collections. In 2006, the total number of exhibitions amounted to nearly 10,000, with 150 million visitors.

孔子学院

Confucius Institute

Borrowing the experience of teaching their national language of the UK, Germany, France and Spain, the Chinese government opened the Confucius Institute in 2004, a nonprofit institute which aims to promote the Chinese language and culture. By the end of 2006, the China National Office for Teaching Chinese as a Foreign Language (Han Ban for short) had received applications from more than 400 agencies in over 60 countries. The Confucius Institute offers Chinese-language courses, training and teaching resources for teachers of Chinese, hosting Chinese-language proficiency tests, issuing certificates to Chinese-language teachers, providing information on China's education, culture, economy and society, and carrying out studies on contemporary China. The Institute actively conducts international cooperation between universities and governments, and between foreign and Chinese enterprises.

Since the first overseas branch of the Confucius Institute opened in South Korea in November 2004, branches have been set up in many parts of Asia, Africa, Europe and America. By the end of February 21, 2008, there were 231 overseas branches – 67 in Asia, 82 in Europe, 56 in North America, 18 in Africa and seven in Oceania. The Institute is supported by 91 domestic universities and 231 overseas universities and agencies. The influence of the Confucius Institute has contributed to the recent rapid growth all over the world in interest in learning Chinese language.

祭孔

Confucius

Confucius is regarded as the greatest ancient thinker, educator and philosopher in China. His thoughts have exerted a tremendous influence on China's history and culture. The rulers of many dynasties held grand ceremonies to worship Confucius, while offering sacrifices to Heaven and their ancestors. The 1980s witnessed the revival of interest in Confucius on China's mainland. In 2005, Confucius' descendants from all over the world gathered in Qufu, Shandong Province, the birthplace of Confucius, to hold the first global ceremony in honor of Confucius. September 28, 2006, the 2,557th anniversary of Confucius' birth, saw ceremonies held in temples of Confucius throughout the world. Among them, the largest ones, called "2006 Grand Ceremonies Honoring Confucius Across the Taiwan Straits," were held in Qufu and Taipei.

Also in 2006, the Chinese government established an educational award named after Confucius under the auspices of UNESCO. The award is offered to outstanding government offices, non-governmental organizations and individuals in the field of education. This is the first UNESCO award sponsored by China.

文物回流
Return of Cultural Relics to China

In recent years, there has been a rising tendency for cultural relics to be returned to China from all over the world. According to UNESCO statistics, among the collections of 200-odd museums in 47 foreign countries, 1.67 million cultural relics originated from China. At present, the number of cultural relics returned to China is 20,000 annually, but at least ten million are still being held overseas. There are three ways for cultural relics to return: recovery through an international legal judgment, gifts in return, and counter-purchase.

Since 2002, the Chinese government has set up a special

fund to recover important national cultural relics, amounting to 50 million yuan (about US$ 6.25 million) annually. The Law on Cultural Relics Protection, revised in October 2002, allows the general public to obtain cultural relics through purchase and auction, thereby encouraging the recovery of national treasures. In May 2006, China's first group for recovering national treasures, consisting of 20 members and organized by the Chinese Foundation for Recovering Cultural Relics from Overseas, brought back a score of cultural relics from Japan. Auction and counter-purchase have become major ways to reclaim lost cultural relics. In fact, over 50 percent of auctioned items in China are Chinese cultural relics from overseas, especially calligraphy and porcelain from the Ming and Qing dynasties.

文化扶贫

Poverty Alleviation in the Aspect of Culture

Impoverished areas should be not only supported economically, but improved intellectually. Poverty alleviation should be realized not only materially, but also in the moral, intellectual and cultural spheres. The Ministry of Culture decided to establish a poverty-alleviation committee in the aspect of culture in December 1993.

These poverty-alleviation projects include constructing libraries exchanging business information via television, giving theatrical performances to children in rural areas, and sending free newspapers and periodicals to the countryside.

环境保护

Environmental Protection

环境友好型社会

Environmentally Friendly Society

The United Nations Conference on Environment and Development (UNCED), passed Agenda 21 in Rio de Janeiro in 1992, which mentions the concept of "environmental soundness" more than 200 times, and proposes the "environmentally friendly" concept. Since then, environmentally friendly technology and products have been greatly promoted and developed. An environmentally friendly society is a society in which people and nature develop harmoniously. Harmony between people as well as between people and society is promoted through harmony between people and nature. Such a society is a social system, which, based on environmental bearing capability, centered on natural laws, and driven by green technology, advocates environmental culture and ecological civilization in order to achieve coordinated development among economy, society and the environment.

Since 1995, a series of activities have been launched to construct environmentally friendly model cities, and ecological demonstration areas, towns, enterprises, schools and communities. By November 2005, China had recognized nine ecological provinces, 528 ecological demonstration areas, 79 environmentally beautiful towns, 50 model cities or districts, 17 industrial eco-parks of various kinds, 32 environmentally friendly enterprises, 499 state-level "green schools," and 2,300 provincial and municipal "green communities."

宜居城市

Livable City

China's State Council has given Beijing, the country's capital, the titles of "international city," "culturally renowned city" and "livable city." The last designation plays down the role of Beijing as an economic center, and praises it as a "livable city." Many other Chinese cities too are striving to reach the "livable" standard. A survey conducted by *Business Watch* magazine and Horizon Research in late 2004 indicated that for the general public, convenience in transportation, cleanness, tidiness and air quality are important standards for judging whether a city is a livable one or not.

Released at the same time was the list of China's livable cities, in which Shanghai came out top, and Dalian and Beijing took the second and third places, respectively, followed by Guangzhou, Chengdu, Qingdao, Hangzhou, Guilin, Zhuhai and Xiamen. In April 2006, the Ministry of Construction approved a project entitled "Scientific Evaluation of the Index System for Livable Cities," signaling that the appraisal and selection of livable cities is to be conducted in a scientific way. The system consists of three categories. The first includes six aspects, i.e., social morality, economic prosperity, environmental beauty, resource bearing, convenience of life and public security. Each aspect contains a number of indices, which are given values.

保护母亲河
Protecting the Mother River

In 1998, the worst flooding for a century occurred in the valleys of the Yangtze, Nenjiang, and Songhua rivers. The protection of the Mother River raised tremendous concern. In 1999, the Communist Youth League, the Environment and Resources Protection Commission under the National People's Congress, the Ministry of Water Resources and the State Environmental Protection Bureau joined hands with other four ministries to implement the plan of "Protecting the Mother River." This plan aims to protect the valleys of several major rivers, including the Yellow and Yangtze rivers. The plan advocates the consciousness of green civilization, sponsors green projects in ecologically degenerated areas (mostly in poor regions), and promotes the country's ecological construction as a whole. The program urges people to donate five yuan to plant a tree and 200 yuan to start planting a 0.06-hectare forest.

Since 1999, the plan has launched eight key projects in regions such as Chongqing and Gansu through which the Yangtze and Yellow rivers pass. In September 2004, six afforestation projects, including that of Dashagou, covered 10,000 ha with trees, and the project moved into new stages of forest manage-

Elementary school students draw pictures with the theme "protecting the mother river, our home garden."

ment and protection as well as afforestation. More than 100,000 young people have taken part in this work. Since the initiation of the protection of the Mother River project, over 300 million people have been mobilized, 300 million yuan raised, and 1,196 model afforestation projects, totaling 275,000 ha, have been completed.

生态省建设

Eco-province Construction

In 2000, the State Council promulgated the Outline for China's Ecological Protection, which proposes eco-construction at each administrative level. An eco-province is one in which coordinated development is achieved among the ecological environment, society and the economy, and sustainable development goals are reached in various categories. That is to say, we are striving to build well-off provinces with a good ecological balance, strong economic competitiveness, excellent environment, and high standard of social morality. Eco-province construction coordinates regional economic development, social progress and environmental protection.

The year 1999 saw the first eco-province construction, in Hainan Province. Now, trials in eco-province construction have been carried out in other provinces, such as Jilin, Heilongjiang, Fujian, Zhejiang, Shandong and Anhui. In September 2006, Sichuan Province took the initiative to start eco-province construction in China's western region. The entire province is divided into seven functional areas. Five systems — ecological economy, ecological environment, ecological culture, ecological society and ecological building capability — are promoted according to different areas and categories. Eco-province construction has been made an important criterion for appraising government performance at each level. Information involving the discharge of pollutants, energy consumption, water resource consumption and environmental security is released regularly every six months. This has also become a standard for evaluating the performance of cadres in the Communist Party of China as well as government officials.

自然保护区

Nature Reserves

China's first nature reserve was the Dinghushan Mountain Nature Reserve, set up in 1956 in Zhaoqing, Guangdong Province. The Sanjiangyuan Nature Reserve, established in August 2000, is China's largest, totaling 316,000 sq km. It is also the highest, with an average elevation of over 4,000 m, and the most bio-diversified. Lying in the hinterland of Qinghai-Tibet Plateau, the Sanjiangyuan Nature Reserve is situated at the junction of the sources of the Yangtze, Yellow and Lancang rivers.

By the end of 2006, China had constructed 2,371 nature reserves of various types and levels. The total area surpassed 1.5 million sq km, accounting for 15 percent of the country's total. These nature reserves protect 88 percent of the country's land ecology types, 87 percent of its wild animal species, 65 percent of its advanced plant groups, nearly 20 percent of its natural forests, 50 percent of its marshes, habitats for over 300 rare wild animals and the main distribution areas of over 130 kinds of trees. The nature reserves also protect geological sites. Twenty-seven nature reserves, including those of Wolong and Jiuzhaigou in Sichuan Province, Mount Changbai in Jilin Province, Mount Dinghu in Guangdong Province and Baishui River in Gansu Province, are on UNESCO's "World Biosphere Reserve" list.

蓝天计划

Blue Sky Plan

"Blue Sky" days are days when the air quality reaches or is better than level II. Since the Blue Sky Plan was promulgated in 1998, Beijing has drastically reduced the density of various pollutants in the air by means of clean energy and energy-saving technology, such as natural gas, electric heaters, ground source heat pump (GSHP) and building energy saving. By the end of 2007, Beijing had 246 "Blue Sky" days, up from 100 in 1998.

The 2005 *Beijing Environment Gazette*, released by the Beijing Municipal Bureau of Environmental Protection, showed that there were decreases of 9.1 percent, 7 percent, 9.1 percent, and 4.7 percent, respectively in the density of sulfur dioxide, nitrogen dioxide, carbon monoxide and inhalable particulate matter in the air, as compared with the previous year. In addition, in 2005 there were only four sandstorm days, much fewer than in previous years; and nine days of level-four pollution, eight days fewer than the previous year.

两控区

Two Control Zones

In January 1998, the State Council approved the Zoning Strategy for Acid Rain and Sulfur Dioxide Control Zones, and set targets for controlling pollution from acid rain and sulfur dioxide. The two control zones involve 175 cities in 27 provinces, autonomous regions and municipalities directly under the central government, covering a total area of 1.09 million sq km and accounting for 11.4 percent of the country's total territory. The control zones for acid rain and sulfur dioxide are 0.8 million and 0.29 million sq km, respectively.

China adjusts the energy structure within the two zones, and promotes the use of clean fuels and low-sulfur coal. Residents in large and medium-sized cities are forbidden to use loose coal for cooking. As compared with 1998, the cities in the sulfur-dioxide control zone with a satisfactory annual average density of sulfur oxide increased from 32.8 percent to 45.2 percent in 2005. For the acid rain control zone, the cities whose annual average density of sulfur dioxide exceeded national level III dropped from 15.7 percent to 4.5 percent. The targets for the two control zones are: The discharge of sulfur dioxide will be held under 14 million tons and the density of sulfur dioxide in cities will reach the national environmental standard by 2010.

黄标车

Yellow-label Vehicles

Yellow-label vehicles refer to those with high emissions of exhaust gas. These vehicles, whose license plates were issued before 1995, cannot meet the European Emission Standard I owing to their backward emission control technology, and thus have been given yellow environmental labels. Tests show that the volume of pollutants an old or dilapidated vehicle discharges is five to ten times as much as that of a new vehicle.

Beijing was the first city in China to enact the yellow and

green environmental labeling system. Green-label vehicles are those whose emissions meet European emission standards I or II. Beijing did not force yellow-label vehicles off the road, but has taken some measures to control their emissions. Yellow-label vehicles should be tested twice a year for emission, and should only travel in restricted zones and time periods, while green-label vehicles are subject to no such restrictions. Since November 2003, yellow-label vehicles have been forbidden to travel on main roads, and should undergo the renovation. Since July 1, 2005, Beijing has supplied gasoline that complies with the National Standard III, tightened vehicle management, and upgraded or eliminated old or dilapidated taxis as well as diesel-powered public buses. Before the 2008 Olympic Games, Beijing will eliminate all the present yellow-label vehicles.

渤海碧海行动计划

Bohai Blue Sea Action Plan

The Bohai Blue Sea Action Plan, approved by the Chinese government in 2001, is an ocean-environment protection plan, aimed at controlling pollution in the Bohai Sea, and restoring its once-fine ecological environment. The 427 projects in the plan mainly involve urban sewage treatment, ocean pollution emergency measures, shoreline eco-construction, and ship pollution control. The projects cover nearly 230,000 sq km, and involve 13 coastal cities within the jurisdiction of Tianjin city, and Hebei, Liaoning and Shandong provinces, as well as the Bohai Sea area.

The Bohai Sea, off China's northern coast, has an area of 78,000 sq km and an average depth of 18 meters. It has suffered the worst environmental damage of any of the country's offshore waters, as its onshore areas are enjoying rapid economic development. Pollution of the Bohai Sea comes from three land sources, i.e., domestic water, industrial waste water, pesticides and chemical fertilizers. Moreover, leakage of pollutant materials, including waste water, from ships, offshore petroleum exploration and additives in marine culture cause severe pollution as well. In recent years, the worsening ecology of the Bohai Sea has been slowed, with improvement in the water quality, but on the whole, the pollution of the Bohai Sea is still severe. But with the implementation of the Bohai Blue Sea Action Plan, it is hoped that this situation can be quickly changed.

沙尘暴

Sandstorms

A sandstorm is a meteorological phenomenon characterized by the carrying of dust and sand by the wind locally or from other areas at high velocity. In light of the intensity, it is categorized into three levels: sandstorm, blowing sand and floating dust. Sandstorm refers to highly turbid air with horizontal visibility of less than one km. Blowing sand indicates considerably turbid air with one-to-ten-km horizontal visibility. Floating dust refers to air with evenly floating dust in it, and horizontal visibility of less than ten km.

The sources of sandstorms in China derive mainly from degenerated or desertified grasslands, barren farmland, arid lakes and urban construction sites, among which degenerated or desertified grasslands and bare farmlands are the most important sources. The spring of 2006 witnessed an unusual 18 sandstorms in North China, of which five were classified as "strong." Sandstorms tend to sweep south from the Republic of Mongolia through Xinjiang and Inner Mongolia autonomous regions and Gansu Province toward Beijing and Tianjin, and affect most of North China. Environmental protection departments are establishing shelterbelts along these routes.

防沙治沙
Sand Prevention and Control

At present, China has got 1.74 million sq km of desertified land, making up 18.1 percent of the country's total. The sandy areas are those with a relatively lower economic level and deteriorated ecology. Since 2000, China has implemented a series of major ecological construction projects, including the control of sandstorm sources in the Beijing and Tianjin areas, the Three North (Northeast, North China and Northwest) Shelterbelts, and the conversion of pastureland to forests. It has promulgated the Law of Sand Prevention and Control, and issued the National Sand Prevention and Control Plan as well as the Decision on Further Strengthening Sand Prevention and Control.

The third national monitoring survey of desertified land in 2005 indicated that for the first time China experienced a net reduction in such land. The situation has been brought under control, as the previous annual extension of 3,436 sq km turned to an annual shrinkage of 1,283 sq km in terms of desertified land. The National Bureau of Forestry has carried out a project for sand prevention and control across the country, striving to check the extension of desertified land by 2010, achieving a gradual reduction in desertified land on the basis of previous results by 2030, returning the desertified land to farmland, and eventually establishing a balanced ecological system in sand-damage-prone areas by 2050.

退耕还林

Returning Farmland to Forests

Returning farmland to forests is aimed at protecting and improving ecological conditions to achieve gradual afforestation and vegetation restoration on farmland with severe soil erosion, on desertified, salinized, rocky-desertified land, and on the farmland with low and unstable produce. The work of converting farmland to forests started in 1999, and the first experiments were conducted in Sichuan, Shaanxi and Gansu provinces, and then spread to 25 other provinces, autonomous regions and municipalities. Since the implementation of the Regulations on Returning Farmland to Forests in 2003, China had returned a total of 22.97 million ha of farmland to forests by the end of 2005.

Another forest protection measure is artificial afforestation. So far, China has planted a total of 57.45 million ha of such forests, ranking first in the world, with forest coverage of 18.21 percent of its total territory, and has been listed by the United Nations Environment Programme as one of the top 15 countries in the world in terms of the preservation of forests. In 1998 China ordered lumbering to be stopped throughout the country, and in many areas former lumberjacks have become forest rangers. In light of the goal set by the strategic report on China's sustainable development for forestry, China's forest coverage will eventually reach 28 percent of its territory, with a net forest growth of 110 million ha.

三化草地

Three-changes Grasslands

The "Three-changes" refers to the degeneration, desertification and salinization of grasslands. The management of these grasslands is aimed at gradually restoring the vegetation by means of allowing grass growth in enclosed pastures, prohibiting or suspending grazing, rotational grazing in designated areas, constructing grasslands and fodder bases, and promoting livestock-raising in pens. China has nearly 400 million ha of grasslands, making up 41.7 percent of the country's total. The 300 million ha of grasslands in North China have formed a 4,500-km natural green belt, serving as an important ecological protection for most Asian countries including China.

Because of long-term of overgrazing, over-gathering of wild plants, irrational exploitation and frequent pest disasters, degeneration has affected over 90 percent of China's natural grasslands. The worst-degenerated grasslands cover nearly 200 million ha, and the situation is deteriorating, with an annual expansion of two million ha of deteriorated land. The malfunctioning of the ecological system has resulted in a sharp decline of biodiversity as well as frequent occurrences of flood, drought and geological disasters. According to the National Ecological Environment Plan issued in 1998, by 2010 newly planted grass and grasslands will have amounted to 50 million ha; the restored Three-change grasslands will have reached 33 million ha, and 22 million ha of desertified land will have been brought under control; soil erosion on six million ha of land will have been checked; and 6.7 million ha of farmland will have been converted.

三北防护林
The Three-North Shelterbelt

The term "Three-North" refers to Northwest China, North

A section of the Three-North Shelterbelt by the Yuxi River in Yulin City, Shaanxi Province

China and Northeast China, where drought, sandstorms and shortage of rain combine to result in severe losses of water and soil. In November 1978, the Chinese government decided to build the Three-North shelterbelt in Northwest China, the northern part of North China, and the western part of Northeast China. This shelterbelt starts in Binxian County in the east and extends to Uzbel Shankou in the west, a distance of 4,480 km. The shelterbelt is 560 km to 1,460 km wide.

The Three-North Project, which is scheduled for completion in 2050, when the country's forest coverage will have risen from 5.05 percent to 14.95 percent. It is said to be the world's largest ecological project.

Over the past 20 years, the Three-North forest belt, involving 551 counties, banners and cities in 13 provinces and regions, and covering 4.069 million sq km, has primarily formed a basic network of forest belts with a combination of trees, shrubs and grass.

绿色出行
Green Commuting

Due to the sharp rise in the number of vehicles in China's cities, a series of problems such as energy consumption, air pollution and traffic jams are inexorably getting worse. The percentages of carbon monoxide, hydrocarbon, nitrogen oxide and fine particles discharged from vehicles in large cities like Beijing, Shanghai and Guangzhou are 80 percent, 75 percent, 68 percent and 50 percent, respectively, and are now the major sources of pollution in these cities. Transportation measures that can save energy, improve energy efficiency, reduce pollution, enhance health and emphasize efficiency are being encouraged and the campaign is called "green commuting."

In large cities like Beijing, people are being encouraged to make more use of public transport means, such as the subway, light rail and public buses; and to form car pools. Walking and cycling are also being encouraged as much as possible. On June 5, 2006, the World Environment Day, the largest public welfare activity in Beijing's history — "green commuting, no car one day per month" — was launched, with the participation of 250,000 people. Similar activities have also been held in Chengdu and Shenzhen. Beijing at present has over three million automobiles, and this figure is growing. It is estimated that if each automobile stopped running one day a month, the total volume of pollution could be reduced by more than 44,000 tons a year.

绿色消费
Green Consumption

Green consumption has three aims: First, to promote unpolluted and health-promoting consumer products; second, to direct more attention to waste disposal during the process of consumption; and third, to guide consumers to change their habits toward consumption, admire Nature and pay more attention to environmental protection, and resource and energy conservation.

In 2006, China made major adjustments and supplements to consumption taxes, aiming at raising the tax rate on such products as large cars, disposable wooden chopsticks and solid wooden floors, or newly levying taxes on items deemed to be environmentally unfriendly. Green products are hazard-free, unpolluted products which cause less environmental pollution during the manufacturing stage, contribute to health in the utilization stage, and are easy to recycle and dispose in the discarded stage. At present, nearly 200 enterprises, 40-odd categories and 500-odd kinds of products have been granted the China Environment Label. Half of these products are closely connected with the people's daily lives.

绿色食品
Green Food

China proposed the concept of green food in 1989. In 1990, it started to develop green food, and set up a green food management agency known as the China Green Food Development Center. Work on green food base construction, and standards for green food and its export are being carried out gradually. The green food label bears three symbols — the sun at the top, and a bud and leaves below.

In recent years, China's agricultural food safety has improved markedly. Three types of certified agricultural products — hazard-free agricultural products, green food and organic food — have been developed. Hazard-free agricultural products are those that meet the country's compulsory standards regarding technical regulations for production, the environment in the place of manufacture, the use of agricultural inputs and product quality. Green food refers to edible agricultural products and processed products which are unpolluted, safe for the health and excellent in quality, and which are manufactured in accordance with the required technical standards, have good environment in the place of manufacture, and the entire manufacturing process of which is strictly controlled. Organic food comprises agricultural products which are manufactured in accordance with organic agricultural means, without the use of inputs such as pesticide, veterinary medicine, fertilizer and additives, and without the adoption of biogenetic technology. By the end of 2005, the number of certified hazard-free agricultural products had reached 16,704 across the country; the number of green-food enterprises totaled 3,695, and that of certified products 9,728, with annual exports hitting US$1.62 billion-worth, and with 6.53 million ha of farmland, grassland, forest and water bodies under supervision. There are 416 certified organic-food enterprises, turning out 1,249 products from 1.66 million ha of certified land. Their exports are worth US$ 136 million a year.

黑色食品
Black Food

In the late 1980s, the main laboratory for functional food

research under the Ministry of Agriculture proposed for the first time the concepts of white food, red food, purple food, yellow food and black food. It specified black food as health-enhancing food, which has a deep natural color and a rational structure of components, is rich in nutrition, and is processed in a scientific way. At present, China has over 100 kinds of black food, and 300 enterprises producing such food, with an annual production value of more than five billion yuan. The so-called black food mainly refers to *semen sesami nigrum*, black rice, dateplum persimmon, black bean, black fungus, kelp, black mushroom, black moss, black-bone chicken and fermented soybeans. Purple food includes purple grape, purple eggplant and purple cabbage. Red food includes chili, onion, red date, tomato, sweet potato, haw, apple and strawberry. Yellow food refers to such food as carrot, soybean, peanut and apricot. White food includes white gourd, muskmelon, bamboo shoot, cauliflower and lettuce.

白色污染
White Pollution

Large quantities of waste plastic packaging, such as agricultural film, plastic film, plastic bags and disposable tableware, do great harm to the natural scenery and environment. Because most of the waste plastic packaging is white, such pollution is called "white pollution." China has become one of the world's ten major manufacturers and consumers of such plastic products. The recycling of waste plastics has become a hot environmental issue in recent years. Data show that China annually consumes 45 billion pairs of throw-away chopsticks, which requires the chopping down of 25 million trees and reduces the country's forest area by two million sq m. Over 12 billion disposable plastic food containers are used each year, and, on average, each person throws away ten.

In the late 1980s, with the pace of the "green revolution" accelerating, "green packaging" came into use. China's green packaging campaign was launched in 1993. The so-called green packaging is hazard-free, environment-friendly packaging which can be recycled or reused so as to curb white pollution. At present, wasted packaging tops 15 million tons a year in China, with a considerably low recycling rate; for example, only 9.6 percent of plastics, and no more than 15 percent of used paper and cardboard are recycled. In the daily garbage, plastic food containers and plastic bags alone account for nearly 1,000 tons.

In June 2008, the government required that since then no supermarket, shopping center, country fair and other retail places were allowed to provide plastic bags in order to reduce the white pollution.

旅游 假日

Tourism and Holidays

黄金周

Golden Week

In September 1999, the State Council set up a new holiday scheme, extending the three most important holidays in the Chinese people's life — Spring Festival, International Labor Day, and National Day to seven days. (Starting from 2008, the Labor Day holiday is reduced to 3 days.) Thus, the concept of "Golden Week" cropped up. Golden Week has boosted domestic demand, stimulated consumption, and offered time for entertainment. However, it has also caused problems of traffic jams and congestion at scenic spots as well. Readjusting the legal holidays and reforming "Golden Week" were the focus of deputies to the National People's Congress (NPC) and Chinese People's Political Consultative Conference (CPPCC) held in 2007.

At present, there are 114 public holidays every year in China. People use them to go sightseeing, and engage in sports, and cultural and commercial activities. Gradually, people are learning to use their expanded leisure time in more creative ways.

出境游

Outbound Travel

In 2001, over 12 million Chinese people traveled oversees, and this number increased to 34.52 million in 2006 – a 280% growth in five years. Having more outbound tourists than Japan, China is now the largest tourist source in Asia. In 2006, 15 countries and regions started to actively develop this market for their own tourism. China has so far approved 132 countries and regions as destinations for outbound tourism. The World Travel

Organization predicts that in 2020 China will be the fourth largest source of tourists in the world, and about 100 million Chinese people will travel abroad annually from then on.

Moreover, Chinese outbound tourists are no longer exclusively from the high-to-middle income group. Households with monthly incomes of 5,000-30,000 yuan each comprise the main body of outbound travelers to neighboring countries. Statistics show that outbound tourists spend far more on shopping and entertainment than on eating, accommodation and traveling. Sightseeing tours are giving way to self-organized and relaxation tours. At present, the main destinations of Chinese mainland tourists are Hong Kong, Macao and Southeast Asia, while Europe and Australia are attracting more and more attention.

71 tourists of the first group to the US organized by Beijing Kanghui Tourist Agent are waiting at the Beijing International Airport for Los Angles.

红色之旅
Red Tourism

A destination of Beijing's Red Tourism — Peking University Red Mansion

"Red Tourism" refers to trips to places associated with the Communist Party of China (CPC) in the period when it led the Chinese people in the revolutionary, Anti-Japanese War and Liberation War periods (1921-1949).

In 2006, to mark the 85th anniversary of the founding of the CPC and to support "Red Tourism," the Ministry of Railways arranged to run 85 special trains to such destinations; and opened special windows to handle student group tickets. According to the *Outline of the 2004-2010 National Red Tourism Development Plan*, the growth rate of people participating in "Red Tourism" will be 15% during the period 2004-2007, and reach

18% during 2008-2010; there will be 12 "key Red Tourism routes," 30 "recommended tours of the country's revolutionary heritage" and 100 "classic red tourist destinations." Meanwhile, old revolutionary base areas will be further developed to accommodate more tourists, the comprehensive income from Red Tourism will hit 100 billion yuan in 2010, the number of people directly employed in this sector will be two million, and another ten million will be indirectly employed.

假日经济

Holiday Economy

The Golden Week has become a new focus of the Chinese economic life, and the holiday economy has also become a hot topic. During the Golden Week between 1999 to 2005 (not including the Spring Festival), there were 1.07 billion people going on sightseeing trips all over the country; there were 3,570 million people going on domestic sightseeing trips during the three Golden Week holidays in 2006, bringing tourist revenue of 623 billion yuan that year. The Golden Week holiday system has played an active role in stimulating consumption, promoting the development of service trades including traffic, accommodation and catering, as well as of related industries. Besides, traditional holidays including the New Year's Day, Lantern Festival and Middle-autumn Festival, theme holidays including the "Valentine's Day" and "Women's Day", have brought a lot of opportunities for sales promotion to businessmen. In China, the holiday economy has become one of the most active and potential factors affecting the national economy.

At present, culture is playing a more and more important role in the holiday economy, the most direct reflection of which is that various cultural, educational and entertainment activities have become the popular way of consumption of people in the holiday economy. Going to museums, watching films, visiting temple fairs, going to libraries and participating in culture festivals, have replaced traveling and shopping. Tourism, catering and related industries in the holiday economy also play the culture card. Many scenic areas use all means to develop tourist products concerning Chinese traditional culture to attract visitors. Cultural consumption has stamped the holiday economy with the brand of "culture," showing that the holiday economy is turning mature.

自助游

Independent Travel

Independent travel, without the help of guides, are becoming fashionable in China nowadays. During the week-long International Labor Day holiday in 2006, over 70% of Beijing residents who traveled for pleasure during that time chose independent travel.

Based on the *Report on Tourist Trends in the Summer of 2006* by the research institute of the Ministry of Commerce, there are three main reasons for choosing independent travel: being able to arrange one's own schedule, being able to shop and eat at one's pleasure, and having more free time. According to the report, the planned expenditure of 65.4% of tourists going abroad was above 10,000 yuan, while that of 82.5% of domestic travelers was below 4,000 yuan. The report also indicated that for independent tourists the top five domestic tourist destinations were Beijing, Hangzhou and Shanghai cities, and Yunnan and Shandong provinces. The first choice for those who wish to travel abroad was Hong Kong and Macao, taking 24.14%, with

Thailand, Australia, France and South Korea ranking second to fifth, respectively.

工业旅游

Industrial Tourism

Along with the development of international tourism, industrial tourism has become a new attraction, based on the resources of manufacture scene, high-technology manufacture facilities, factory environment and enterprise culture. Industrial tourism originated in France in the 1950s, starting with the automotive industry and radiating to other industries.

At the beginning of 1999, the Haier Group, China's largest enterprise making household appliances, introduced industrial tourism to China when it established the Haier International Travel Agency. It received 240,000 visitors that year. In 2005, the National Tourism Administration designated 103 "experimental units of industrial tourism," showing that industrial tourism has formally entered the market operation phase.

乡村游

Rural Tourism

Rural tourism areas receive over 300 million people annually, bringing revenue of more than 40 billion yuan. China plans to set up 100 counties, 1,000 townships and 10,000 villages specializing in rural tourism by 2010. The National Tourism Administration set rural tourism as the theme of the 2006 China Tourism Year, with the slogan of "New countryside, new tourism, new experience, and new fashion."

Rural tourism, featuring rural life, customs and scenery, includes "enjoying flowers in spring, plowing and weeding in summer, and picking fruits in autumn." In addition, people can live in a farmer's home, eat farm food and do farm work."

As a new type of eco-tourism, rural tourism is being developed on a large scale in China, including sightseeing farms, agricultural parks, rural educational parks, forest parks and folk-customs villages.

Tourists are watching a big waterwheel at a displaying area of the Beautiful Countryside of Jingguan Township, Beibei District, Chongqing.

修学游

Study Tourism

Study tourism emerged in China in 2003. The current study tour products include "parents and children trips," "sightseeing summer camps," "theme travel" and "finding ways to study abroad." "Parents and children trips" aim to build communication bridges between parents and children, enhancing family cohesiveness. Cartoon study tours have been offered recently, and other themes include "loving care study tours," "carrying one kilogram more" and "entering mountains." Scenic areas, including Jiuzhaigou, Mount Huangshan and Guilin, and seaside cities are the main focuses of study tourism. Some travel agencies also offer "famous universities tours."

Since outbound travel is becoming more and more available, many students and their parents want to go abroad to widen their horizons. There are tours which take people to famous foreign universities to meet local students, besides the conventional sightseeing. Particularly popular are "homestay tours," during which students stay in the homes of local residents, to experience the local lifestyle and learn a foreign language in a favorable environment. Japan, Korea, European countries and Australia are the main destinations of study tourism.

探险游

Adventure Tourism

In recent years, adventure tourism has boomed, including traveling on foot, mountaineering, rafting and pony trekking. Routes include the Silk Road, Tianshan Mountains, Taklimakan, and Lop Nor – all in Xinjiang Uygur Autonomous Region.

Adventure tours are not ordinary traveling. They demand physical and psychological preparation, and rational prediction of ailments and accidents. At present, problems existing in adventure tourism are poor safety awareness and inefficient management. To remedy this situation, the National Tourism

Administration is calling for the enhancement of safety education among the public.

文明旅游

Civilized Traveling

On August 8, 2006, the Committee for the Guidance of Civilized Behavior issued the Action Plan for Improving Chinese Travelers' Behavior. The committee criticized the uncivilized behavior of some Chinese travelers abroad, including slovenliness, impoliteness, disorderliness, paying no attention to hygiene, environment and public facilities, and being noisy.

Following this, the Central Civilization Work Office and the National Tourism Administration issued the *Guide to Civilized Behavior for Chinese Outbound Travelers* and *Civilized Behavior Pledge for Chinese Domestic Travelers.*

春晚

Spring Festival Gala

This Spring Festival party presented by China Central Television (CCTV) has been broadcast live on the eve of the Chinese New Year every year since 1983. It includes singing, dancing, comedy acts and conjuring tricks. In China, New Year's Eve is the most important occasion in the year for family reunions, and in 2005, the Spring Festival Gala was watched by 94.5% of Chinese families. Appearing in the Spring Festival Gala is considered a career boost for young performers.

春运
Transport During the Spring Festival

The Spring Festival, or the Chinese lunar New Year, is a traditional festival celebrated most solemnly in China. Every year, millions of people scattered all over the country and abroad go home for family reunions. From 1997 to 2006, the flow of people during the Spring Festival increased by nearly one hundred million persons annually, mainly because the migrant worker population had grown to 140 million and the student population to 23 million. So transportation during the Spring Festival is a big problem.

During the 2006 Spring Festival, 2.054 billion people traveled by road, rail, water and air in a space of 40 days.

台商春节包机
Charter Flights for Taiwan Compatriots

The proposal for Spring Festival charter flights between the Taiwan Straits was raised by Taiwanese businessmen and some eminent persons in the island province in 2002. There are no direct flights across the Taiwan Straits. In the following year, the first Spring Festival charter flights for Taiwan businessmen were arranged. The Taiwan authorities insisted that the flights stop in Hong Kong or Macao en route; and only Taiwan airlines could operate the charter flights. Also, the planes were not allowed to take passengers back, and the mainland terminal was restricted to Shanghai. In 2004, the program was suspended because of obstacles put up by the Taiwan authorities. But in 2005, airlines from both sides of the Straits operated round-trip and non-stop charter flights for the Spring Festival. It was the first time that civil airliners had crossed the Straits for 56 years. Besides Shanghai, Beijing and Guangzhou operated the flights. The Spring Festival charter flights for Taiwanese businessmen in 2006 made following breakthroughs: They were available not only for Taiwan businessmen and their relatives but also for any other Taiwan resident, and Xiamen was added to the list of terminals on the mainland. In addition, the number of flights was increased.

The next breakthrough came on September 29, 2006, when the first charter flights for Taiwan businessmen for the Mid-Autumn Festival were inaugurated. A total of 24 airliners from six airline companies representing both sides of the Taiwan Straits completed 48 flights, transporting about 10,000 Taiwan compatriots.

庙会

Temple Fairs

Temple fairs have a long history in China. On certain Buddhist sacrificial days, major temples are the venues for all kinds of feasting and other entertainment activities.

Suppressed during the "cultural revolution" (1966-1976), temple fairs have seen a revival since the policies of reform and opening-up were introduced some 30 years ago. People have come to see traditional culture in a new light, and the government has enhanced protection of it. Moreover, traditional customs on display at temple fairs attract many foreign visitors. Temple fairs in fact play an active role in promoting the local economy, stimulating the interflow of commodities between town and country, and the development of tourism.

A girl is selecting a tiger pillow at the Beijing Temple of Earth Fair during Spring Festival.

社会

Society

人口普查

Population Census

Population censuses are conducted at regular times in a unified way, involving door-to-door inquiries. The censuses aim to find out the Chinese population's number, structure and distribution, as well as its social, economic and cultural characteristics. The census work includes data gathering, evaluation, analysis and research of materials, and publicity.

There have been five censuses since New China was founded in 1949. The first was held on June 30, 1953, when the population was found to be 594.35 million (not including the populations of Hong Kong, Macao and Taiwan, same below). The second was held on June 30, 1964, revealing a total population of 694.58 million. The third was held on July 1, 1982, revealing a total population of 1,008.18 million. The fourth was held on July 1, 1990, revealing a total population of 1,133.68 million. The fifth was held on November 1, 2000, revealing a total population of 1,265.83 million.

少数民族

Ethnic Minorities

China is a unified multi-ethnic country, consisting of 56 ethnic groups. The Han accounts for 91.6% of the country's total population, and so the other 55 ethnic groups are often referred to as ethnic minorities. According to the fifth census, conducted in 2000, 18 of these ethnic minorities had a population of over one million, namely the Zhuang, Manchu, Hui, Miao, Uygur, Yi, Tujia, Mongol, Tibetan, Puyi, Dong, Yao,

Young people of the Yi nationality celebrate the New Year as well as welcome villagers and visitors, by blowing traditional trumpets.

Korean, Bai, Hani, Li, Kazak and Dai. Of these, the Zhuang had the largest population, with 16.179 million. Seventeen ethnic minorities had populations of fewer than one million, namely, the She, Lisu, Gelao, Lagu, Dongxiang, Va, Sui, Naxi, Qiang, Tu, Xibo, Mulao, Kirgiz, Daur, Jingpo, Sala and Maonan; 20 ethnic minorities had populations of between 10,000 and 100,000, namely, the Blang, Tajik, Pumi, Achang, Nu, Ewenke, Jing, Jino, De'ang, Uzbek, Russian, Yugur, Bonan, Monba, Oroqen, Derung, Tatar, Hezhen, Gaoshan (not including the Gaoshan people living in Taiwan) and Lhoba. The last had the smallest population — only 2,965.

The Han is distributed all over the country, and is especially numerous on the middle and lower reaches of the Yellow, Yangtze and Pearl rivers, as well as the Northeast Plain. The 55 ethnic minorities are widely dispersed and found on 64.3% of the total area of the country. Most of them live in the border areas of northeast, north, northwest and southwest China.

Yunnan Province is home to the most ethnic minorities –23, and Xinjiang has 15.

The ethnic minorities, under unified state leadership, practise regional autonomy in areas where they live in concentrated communities, with organs of self-government to exercise the power of autonomy and administer their internal affairs.

计划生育

Family Planning

With a huge population but relatively little farmland, China has been implementing a strict family planning policy since the 1970s, combining central guidance and voluntary participation. Governments at all levels provide consultation, guidance and technical services for all couples in the spheres of reproduction and care for babies.

China's current family planning policy encourages late marriage, late birth, and fewer but healthier births. Couples are encouraged to have only one child. In rural areas, couples may have second baby in exceptional cases, but must wait several years after the birth of the first child. In areas inhabited by minority peoples, each ethnic group is free to enact related regulations in accordance with its traditions and economic situation.

经济适用房

Affordable Housing

Affordable housing is a new type housing policy introduced by the government in the process of housing reform, to meet the needs in the social and economic development. Suiting middle- and low-income families, this type of housing is offered by the government at a lower price than the market price. The former application standard for affordable housing was an annual family income of less than 60,000 yuan, but since November 5, 2007, new application standard has been implemented: The annual family income of the households with one, two, three, four or five family members is less than 22,700 yuan, 36,300 yuan, 45,300 yuan, 52,900 yuan or 60,000 yuan respectively and the net value of total family assets is lower than 240,000 yuan, 270,000 yuan, 360,000 yuan, 450,000 yuan or 480,000 yuan respectively. In addition, the per capita floor space of the family should be less than 10 square meters.

A view of affordable housing in Beijing

商品房

Commercial Housing

Commercial housing refers to residential and commercial buildings and other types of buildings built by real estate developers who have obtained government permission to offer them for sale on the market.

Before 2002, commercial housing had two categories, one for Chinese citizens and the other for foreigners. The first category referred to the residential buildings, commercial housing and other buildings built by real estate developers through the assignment of the right to the use of the land, and examined and approved by the responsible government department to sell to Chinese citizens (not including Hong Kong, Macao and Taiwan). The category referred to the residential buildings, commercial housing and other buildings built by real estate developers through land leasing, and listed by the responsible government department as formal plan to sell domestically and internationally, according to the regulations of responsible foreign investment department. After September 1, 2002 when China became a member of the WTO, this two-category system was abolished.

The price of commercial housing is usually affected by the following factors: cost, tax dues, profit, commission fee, as well as location, storey, exposure, quality, and the price of materials.

房奴

Mortgage Slaves

Mortgage Slaves are people who struggle under the heavy burden of housing mortgage loans. During their 20 to 30 peak years, they spend 40% to 50% or even more of their disposable income on meeting mortgage principle and interest. Thus, housing purchase reduces the amount of money that mortgagees can afford to spend on education, medicine, supporting elders, and so on. The results are a lower quality of life and even a feeling of being enslaved. As house prices have been rising sharply in China, it could take up to 40 years to pay off a housing mortgage loan. Thus, a large number of people have to continue doing jobs they do not like for fearing of losing their income.

In terms of China's present level of economic development, if the percentage of housing expenditure is over 30% of a family's income it is a heavy burden. It is estimated that about 31% of house purchasers in China today have to earmark 50% of their monthly income for mortgage payment, far above the international warning limit. In addition, the People's Bank of China increased the interest on deposits in 2004 and 2006. In this situation, the term Mortgage Slaves has emerged, symptomatic of the real estate bubble.

节能

Energy-saving Residences

According to the data released by the Ministry of Construction, 95% of China's 40 billion sq m of building space consumes too much energy. The building energy consumption accounts for nearly 30% of the country's total energy consumption. To remedy this situation, China's Ministry of Construction now demands that new buildings meet stringent standards concerning energy saving in building industry, including savings in heat, water and electricity supplies. The goal is to save energy of the equivalent of 350 million tons of standard coal by 2020. It is calculated, however, that this will cause an increase in construction costs of only 100-150 yuan per sq m.

The problems to be tackled in this regard include lack of regard for energy conservation on the part of both buyers and developers, and below-standard building materials, technology and installations in energy saving. In addition, energy-saving laws and regulations, and management are not sufficiently enforced.

分配改革

Income Reform

Since the introduction of the reform and opening-up policies in the late 1970s, there have been two rounds of reform in the field of income — one in the 1980s and another launched in July 2006. The reforms concentrated on three aspects: increasing the incomes of poorer people, expanding the moderate-income population and appropriately taxing high-income earners.

上海世博会

World Expo Shanghai

World Expo is a large-scale international exhibition hosted by an individual country and participated by other countries and international organizations, aiming to display the world's latest social, economic, cultural and technological achievements. Since the first one held in London in 1851, the World Expo has become known as the "Olympics of the world's economy, technology and culture." According to the Bureau of International

Expositions (BIE), world expositions are divided into two categories: registered expos (previously called comprehensive expo), lasting six months and held every five years since 2000, and approved expos (previously called professional expos), lasting three months and held between two registered expos.

China participated in a world exposition for the first time in 1982 in Knox William, and established ties with the BIE. On May 3, 1993, the BIE accepted China as its 46th member country. On December 3, 2002, Shanghai won the right to host the 2010 World Expo at the BIE's 132th meeting in Monte Carlo. During the Shanghai Expo, scheduled for May 1 to October 31, 2010, some 200 countries, regions and international organizations will be represented, and 70 million visitors are expected. The theme of Shanghai Expo 2010 is "Making urban life more wonderful." During the expo, Shanghai will demonstrate its multicultural lifestyle, economic prosperity, technical creation, community reconstruction, and exchanges between the city and the countryside.

世界园艺博览会

International Horticultural Expo

International horticultural expositions are held under the auspices of the International Association of Horticultural Producers (AIPH). Known as "the world's gardening festival," the international horticultural exposition displays the latest achievements in this field from all over the world, including exotic flowers and rare herbs.

Kunming, capital city of southwest China's Yunnan Province, hosted the 1999 International Horticultural Expo, with the theme "Man and Nature — Marching Toward the 21st Century." Shenyang, the capital city of China's Liaoning Province, hosted the 2006 World Horticultural Expo.

福布斯中国富豪榜

Forbes List of China's Richest People

Forbes, founded in 1917, publishes over 100 lists of figures, companies and fashion every year. The "richest list" was introduced in 1982, and on October 30, 2003, *Forbes* published its first list of the richest people in China. On "Forbes 2006 China Rich List", 37-age-old Huang Guangyu, founder of the Gome household appliance chain, ranked top with total assets of US$2.3 billion. A quarter of the richest people in China are under 40 years old, showing that a group of multimillionaires have emerged with the boom in the retail, network and real estate sectors over the past ten years.

According to the *2006 Blue Paper on the Private Economy* compiled by the All-China Federation of Industry and Commerce, during the 10th Five-Year Plan period (2001-2005) the private economy became the main channel for industrial investment, employment, taxation, and foreign trade, accounting for more than 75% of the urban and rural employed population. The private economy is now the main source of tax revenues in many parts of the country.

突发公共事件

Public Emergencies

Public emergencies are events which entail significant casualties, property damage, environmental destruction and social disruption, endangering public security. In January 2006, the State Council issued the National Emergency Response Program for Public Incidents, marking the establishment of the framework of an emergency response program. The framework embraces national, special, departmental, regional, and enterprise and public institution emergency response measures. It divides public emergencies into four categories, namely, natural, accident, public health, and public safety emergencies. Emergencies are roughly divided into four levels according to their nature, degree of seriousness, controllability and scope: level I (extremely serious), level II (serious), level III (relatively big) and level IV (ordinary), symbolized by the colors — red, orange, yellow and blue — respectively.

In line with the program, after the occurrence of an extremely serious or serious public emergency, province-level government and related departments of the State Council should report to the State Council within four hours, and give notice to regions and departments concerned. While they are dealing with the situation, they should send timely reports to the State Council. Public emergencies should be made public immediately.

突发公共卫生事件

Public Health Emergencies

In February 2006, the State Council published four special emergency response programs in the case of public health emergencies, namely, the national public health emergency program, national public health rescue program, national emergency program for major animal epidemics, and national emergency program for major food safety incidents. The national public health emergency program deals with major infectious diseases, unknown diseases, major cases of food poisoning and occupational hazards, natural disasters and public security incidents, entailing serious consequences to the public. They are divided into four levels, i.e., extreme (level Ⅰ), major (level II), relatively big (level III) and ordinary (level IV), according to the nature, degree of damage, and scope of the emergency.

In September 2006, the Ministry of Public Health released national public health emergency information for the first time. According to the *Information on Epidemics of Infectious Diseases and Public Health Emergencies*, released by the Ministry in March 2006, information on public health emergencies will be given out every month. Monthly reports concerning infectious diseases had already been started in February 2004.

网上购物

Online Shopping

Along with the popularization of the Internet, online shopping has become a fashionable way of consumption. According to the China Internet Network Information Center, by the end of June 2006, there were 1,230 million Chinese netizens, and several online shopping websites, including Joyo, Dangdang, eBay and Taobao. According to the *Guidelines for Online Trading* issued by the Ministry of Commerce in June 2006, all online shops must be registered with the department of commercial administrations.

E-commerce is playing a more and more important role in extending commerce, reducing costs and improving efficiency. In 2005, the value of China's e-commerce reached 680 billion yuan. However, problems of dishonest trading have emerged in large numbers. In 2005, e-commerce complaints were the second most numerous of all complaints received by the China Consumers' Association. To meet this situation a network trust system has been put in place, with safety certification standards and online payment methods laid down in the *Electronic Signature Law* .

一卡通

All-in-One Card

In January 2007, the National Language Resources Monitoring and Research Center, Beijing Language and Culture University and Communications University of China jointly issued the "Top 10 Popular Terms in China's Media in 2006," among which the "All-in-One Card" was prominent. Various types of these cards, including "All-in-One Traffic Card" and "Campus All-in-One Card" are becoming regular parts of people's life.

An All-in-One Traffic Card system, covering subways, buses and taxis, went into operation on May 10, 2006. At the National People's Congress (NPC) and Chinese People's Political Consultative Conference (CPPCC) sessions in March 2007, a nationwide "All-in-One Card" system for social insurance was proposed. Shandong Province plans to experiment with an "All-in-One Card" system covering transportation, tourism, education, community services, water, electricity, heating, cable television and telephone communication, as well as the sharing of information resources, starting in the cities. Beijing is to introduce an "All-in-One Record" for outpatient services valid at all hospitals. In addition, an "All-in-One Card" system is planned for medical payments and physical examinations, aimed at stopping abuses in medical charges.

霸王条款

Consumer Rights

World Consumer Rights Day is celebrated on March 15 every year. Since 1987, the China Consumers Association and local-level associations have jointly staged publicity activities with departments concerned on that day to educate people on the rights of consumers and knowledge of the law covering the production and consumption of everyday goods. Since 1991, China Central Television (CCTV) has held evening parties on the same day to publicize consumer rights. The 10,000-Mile March for Quality was initiated in 1992 to help standardize market operations and guide consumption. The 10,000 Mile-March for Quality 2006 had four theme teams: city service quality, rural food safety, students' marching for social order and march for urban prosperity. In 1993 the Law for the Protection of Consumers' Rights was promulgated. At present, the quality condition of consumption products in China is still not satisfactory. Complaints about foodstuffs, automobiles and household remodeling were on the list of Top 10 Complaints received by the Promotion Association for the 10,000-Mile March for Quality in 2005.

食品质量安全市场准入制度

Food Quality Market Access System

China has established and implemented a food quality safety market access system since 2001. To be allowed to sell at public markets, foodstuffs must have QS (Quality Safety) certification.

The QS mark was first applied to rice, flour, oil, soy sauce and vinegar, and from May 1, 2003, such items not bearing the QS sign were banned from sale. Later, seven other items were added to the list, namely, meat products, dairy products, beverages, condiments, instant noodles, biscuits and convenience foods. By the end of June 2006, China had brought 15 categories with 370 kinds of foodstuffs into the scope of those needing government approvals for sale at markets. By the end of the year these figures had risen to 28 and 525, respectively.

消费税

Consumption Tax

China started to levy this tax in 1994. At present, there are four categories of items subject to consumption tax: Goods that have the potential to damage health, social order and ecological environment if consumed in excess, for example, tobacco, alcohol and fireworks; luxury items and unnecessary articles for daily consumption, including expensive jewelry and cosmetics; high-energy-consuming goods, including automobiles and motorcycles; and nonrenewable and irreplaceable consumer goods, including gasoline, diesel oil and disposable chopsticks.

On April 1, 2006, China added golf equipment, high-grade watches, yachts, solid wooden flooring to the list of consumption tax items. The category of refined oil products subject to consumption tax was expanded to including gasoline, diesel oil, naphtha, solvent oil, lubricating oil, fuel oil and aviation kerosene, at the same time deleting skin- and hair-protection products from the list. At the same time, the tax rates for liquor, automobiles, motorcycles and tires were adjusted. The highest tax rate for an automobile can reach 20%. Consumption tax plays a useful role in promoting environmental protection and energy saving, and guiding the production and consumption of the goods affected.

个人所得税

Personal Income Tax

China started to levy personal income tax in 1980. From 1994 to 2004, the country's personal income tax revenue increased from 7.3 billion yuan to 173.7 billion yuan, and the proportion of personal income tax revenue in the total tax revenue rose from 1.33% in 1993 to 6.8% in 2004. In 2005, personal income tax revenue hit 200 billion yuan for the first time. From March 1, 2008, income tax deduction increased from 800 yuan to 2,000 yuan per month, aiming to reduce the tax burden on medium- and low-income earners.

The growing personal income tax revenue is mainly a result of the booming economy, income increase, and the standard wage system now carried out by public organs and institutions. Based on unified requirements, various levels of taxation organs organize one or two special inspections of personal income tax every year, focusing on high-income industries and individuals. At present, over 80% of personal income tax revenue comes from withholding. According to the Self-declaration Rules Concerning Individual Income Tax (provisional) issued by the State Administration of Taxation in November 2006, taxpayers shall make tax declarations to the tax authorities in the following five cases: those with annual income of over 120,000 yuan; receiving salary and remuneration from two or more employers in China; generating income abroad; generating taxable income without withholding agent; and other cases as specified by the State Council.

幸福工程

Happiness Project

The Happiness Project — action to relieve impoverished mothers, was founded by the China Population Welfare Foundation, China Family Planning Association and *China Population* in 1995. This project focuses on impoverished mothers of families complying with the family planning policy in poverty-stricken areas. It aims to "cure poverty, cure ignorance and cure illness" by giving small amounts of financial aid and direct personal support. The financial aid amounts to 1,000-3,000 yuan per family.

In addition, the China Foundation for Poverty Alleviation has started a public welfare program under the title "Action 120 for the Safety of Mothers and Babies," to improve the healthcare of poor mothers and babies. It was launched in Lijiang County (present-day Yulong County), Yunnan Province, in September 2000. The number "120" means "1 family, 2 lives, 0 child-bearing risk." This program aims to mobilize the public to go to poverty-stricken areas, experience the life of the people there, and help them improve the local economy. Moreover, the public welfare action program "Love of the Earth, Cisterns for Mothers," initiated by the China Women's Development Foundation, aims to help people, especially women, shake off poverty exacerbated by the severe water shortage in the central and western regions of the country, and raise funds to build cisterns for collecting rainwater.

春雷计划

Spring Buds Program

Illiteracy continues to be a problem in China's poverty-stricken mountainous areas. Some 70% of illiterate people are women, and girls account for two-thirds of the children who are unable to attend school. The "Spring Buds Program" was launched by the China Children and Teenagers' Fund to help young girls who are forced by poverty to drop out of school. It raises funds from all over the world to hold "Spring Buds Girls' Classes" in poverty-stricken areas.

In addition, the "Program for the Safe and Healthy Development of Chinese Children" (known as the Ankang Program for short), jointly initiated by the China Children and Teenagers' Fund and State Administration of Work Safety in May 2000, aims to build a good social atmosphere for children and youngsters, cultivate their skills and promote their healthy development. In May 2003, the "Ankang Campus Program" was initiated, with the theme of "saving children from dropping out of school, from disease, from harm and from crime."

红十字博爱送万家

Universal Love for Thousands of Households

"Universal Love for Thousands of Households" is a program launched by the Chinese Red Cross Foundation (CRCF) to help people in difficult conditions. In 1999, the CRCF began to raise funds for this project, and has been assisted by the National Public Welfare Lottery Fund since 2003. By the end of 2005, the CRCF had collected 132 million yuan and received 16.68 million yuan from the Lottery, which it used to benefit 668,000 poor families, a total of 2.672 million people. Moreover, in 2003, the China Charity Foundation and its member units initiated the "Charity Warms Thousands of Families" activity all over the country, raising funds for destitute households to enjoy the Spring Festival, and distributing money, food and clothing to them. In 2005, they raised 560 million yuan for two million destitute households and families living on basic living allowances.

The CRCF launched the "Red Cross Angel Program" in August 2005, aiming to protect the life and health of farmers and children in poor areas. The program includes the "Red Cross Angel Fund," offering medical relief to poor peasants and their children suffering from serious illnesses, assisting the government to improve medical treatment in poverty-stricken areas and regions inhabited by ethnic minorities, training village medical staff, and encouraging farmers to join the new cooperative medical system.

新长城

New Great Wall

The New Great Wall is a charitable program for destitute university students, run by the China Foundation for Poverty Alleviation and with support from the State Council Leading Group Office for Poverty Alleviation and Development, and the Ministry of Education. Launched in September 2002, this program provides financial aid (mainly for living expenses), and skill training and employment services. By the end of June 2006, it had benefited over 20,000 university students.

In July 2006, a New Great Wall activity with the theme of "my university, your love" was launched, with the aim of assisting poor students to participate in the college entrance examinations that year. The drive focused on 12 key aid-the-poor counties in nine provinces.

夕阳工程

Sunset Project

The "Sunset Project" was launched by the China Charity Foundation. It raises funds from all over the world, providing housing and medical care services for millions of elderly people, in light of the challenges of China's aging society.

By the end of 2005, the population aged 65 or over had reached 100.55 million in China, accounting for 7.7% of the country's total population. The accepted international standard stipulates that a country enters the stage of an aging society when its population over 65 accounts for 7% of the total population or the population over 60 makes up 10% of the total. Based on this standard, China became an aging society in 1999. Now, China has the largest aging population in the world, accounting for one fifth of the total global aging population. Aging in China is imbalanced between regions, with the eastern coastal areas aging quicker than the underdeveloped western areas, and the aging level higher in the rural areas than in the urban areas. Furthermore, aging in China is outstripping the rate of modernization. Developed countries usually enter the stage of an aging society when their per capita GDP is 5,000-10,000 US dollars. However, China's per capita GDP is only 2,000 US dollars now, meaning that the aging population is becoming a strain on the economy.

农民工

Peasant Workers

Peasant workers refer to people from rural areas making a living by working in cities, instead of farming. Most of them engage in physical labor in the construction, heavy and mining industries, and the service industry. Some undertake household management, while others engage in trade. In recent years, there has appeared the phenomenon of a shortage of peasant workers, especially in southern China's Guangdong Province. To counter this trend, local governments and enterprises are drawing up policies to raise peasant workers' wages and improve their working conditions.

Statistics show that there are 20 million children living with their peasant worker parents in cities among the 150 million floating population in China, and 20 million left by their parents at their homes in rural areas. As a result, educational, living, psychological and safety problems concerning these children have emerged. In order to properly solve these problems, the government and relevant departments have adopted many measures, including allowing migrant children to study in urban state-run schools, opening schools specially for migrant children and establishing special working groups to look after the children left behind.

博客

Bloggers

In China, the number of bloggers is increasing rapidly. A survey shows that 6.9% of blog readers believe the entire contents of blogs, 1.5% do not believe, and 64.8% are convinced by most of the contents.

营养师

Nutrition Consultants

Nutrition consultants play an important role in people's

daily life nowadays. They study the relationship between the nutritive elements contained in food and the functions of the human body, and advise people on "what to eat, how to eat, how much to eat." A qualified nutrition consultant should have both medical knowledge and food knowledge. At present, there is only one nutrition consultant for each 500,000 people, but the first draft of China's first nutrition regulations stipulate that dining halls and catering units with over 100 people should be provided with at least one nutrition consultant each.

Since the Ministry of Labor and Social Security started publicizing new occupations in August 2004, seven groups of new occupations have been announced, and 76 new occupations have gained recognition. New occupations include cartoon designer, art or sports agent, car model maker, packaging designer, pet trainer, tea art specialist, wine maker and shoe designer.

亚健康

Sub-health

Sub-health, also called the "third state" or "gray state," is interpreted as a borderline state between health (about 15% of the population) and disease (also 15% of the population). It refers to the physical condition of people who, while not yet ailing, have present in their bodies different degrees of elements which are likely to cause ill-health.

Most sub-healthy people are middle-aged or elderly. The typical symptoms of this condition are hypertension, high blood-pressure, excess body fat and low immunity. Other symptoms include depression, lack of energy and slow reflexes.

It is necessary to improve the lifestyles of sub-healthy people by spreading medical knowledge and encouraging them to ensure that they have a balanced diet, take regular exercise and adopt other wholesome habits.

Sub-health is not a diseased condition. Therefore, the key to recovering from sub-health is not to depend on medicines or treatment by doctors, but on adjusting one's lifestyle

大学生保姆

College Student Housekeepers

Among the over 70 million urban households in China, the demand for housekeeping services is growing, and it is estimated that there is a shortage of over 10 million housekeepers. Furthermore, many households want housekeepers with educational qualifications to provide services including family education, financing, management and secretarial work.

In July 2006, a "summer housekeeper group" consisting of 52 college students from Sichuan Province arrived in Beijing, marking the beginning of 1-3 month-long housekeeping service. They had come from ten institutions of higher learning in Sichuan and with 20 specialties, including English, economic management and housekeeping management. In October 2006, the first housekeeping training class for college students was opened in Chengdu, capital of Sichuan. During the three-week training period, the students had long-distance interviews with employers from all over the country.

421 家庭

421 Families

A "421" family consists of one child, two parents and four

grandparents. It is becoming the main family form of future Chinese society. The only children are those born since the early 1970s, when the family planning policy was enforced nationwide. The major social problem caused by "421" families is the pressure of supporting the older generations. According to a survey covering Beijing, Shanghai and Guangzhou cities, 35% of the families support four old people, and 49% families, two to three old people.

Experts fear that this might undermine the traditional family structure of "four generations living together." Moreover, it will tend to weaken China's long-standing clan network and social ethics, as fewer and fewer people will have cousins, aunts, uncles, brothers or sisters.

空巢家庭

Empty-nest Families

An empty-nest family is one that its children have grown up and left their parents.

Along with urban modernization, the "empty-nest family" phenomenon is becoming increasingly common. For example, in Beijing, "empty nest families" account for 34%. "Empty-nest elders" face difficulties in not having younger family members help them around the house, especially when they are sick. It is suggested that this problem calls for an expansion of public services.

丁克族

DINK

DINK (Double Income, No Kids) is a new phenomenon in

China, as both spouses are breadwinners.

Research carried out in Beijing, Shanghai, Guangzhou and Chengdu cities shows that, among females aged 15-59, 20% "do not want children even after they get married," and this proportion among the young and middle-aged is 24.7%. In contrast, the traditional Chinese family concept stresses the importance of the wife staying at home to look after the children while the husband goes out to work.

黄昏恋

Twilight Romance

Twilight romance refers to love affairs and marriage between elderly people. Such behavior was long considered taboo in China, especially the remarriage of widows. However, along with China's reform and opening-up, people's lifestyles and views on marriage are changing remarkably. The aged have more opportunities to communicate, and the number of elders having "twilight romances" is on the increase. In fact, there are marriage agencies in cities specially serving the aged.

排队推动日

Voluntary Queuing Day

On January 18, 2007, the Beijing Overall Plan for the Activity "Welcoming the Olympics, Improving Manners and Fostering New Attitudes" in 2007 contained in *Document No.2 in 2007* was promulgated by the Capital Cultural and Social Progress Committee at the mobilization meeting for Welcoming the

Olympics, Improving Manners and Fostering New Attitudes. The Plan sets the 11th of each month as "Voluntary Queuing Day," in order to help put an end to uncivilized behavior in public places and improve Beijing's image for the Olympic Games. The number 11 draws people's attention to queuing one by one when two or more people are waiting, hence the choice of the date. The Committee is recruiting volunteers to help people form orderly queues.

体育 奥运会

Sports and the Olympic Games

全民健身

Nationwide Physical Fitness

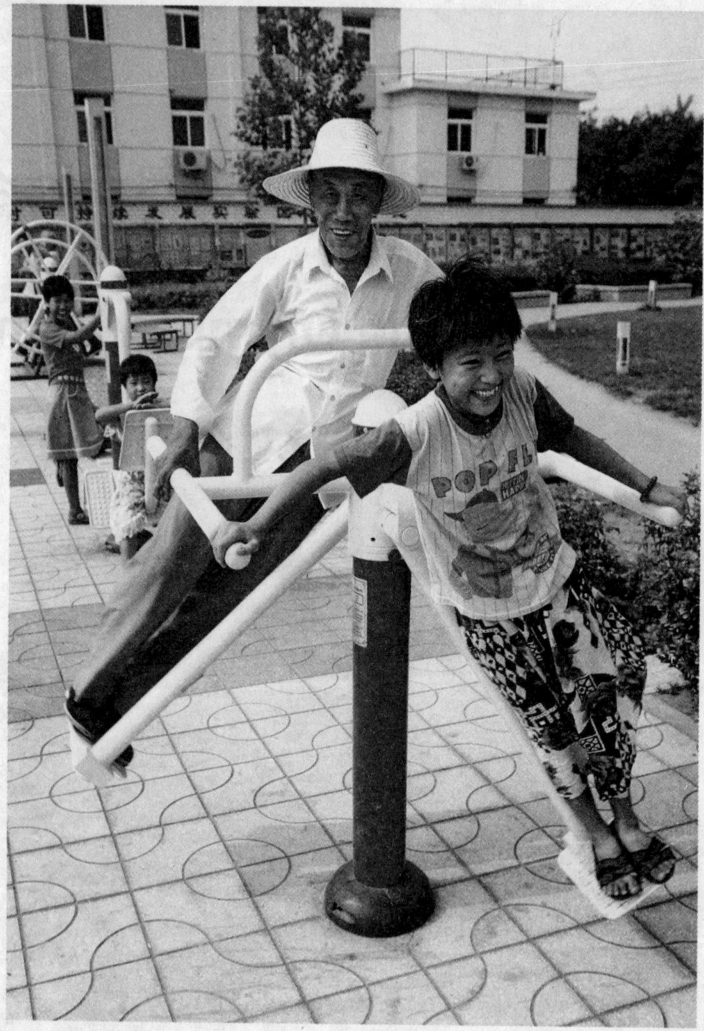

More people in China regardless of age are taking exercises and having fun nowadays.

The Physical Health Law, the first of its type in the People's Republic of China, was adopted in 1995. In the same year, the

State Council promulgated the Nationwide Physical Fitness Program Outline. Aiming to improve the health and overall physical condition of the general population, this program, with the emphasis on young people and children, encourages everyone to engage in at least one sports activity daily, learn at least two ways of keeping fit and have a health examination every year. By the end of 2005, 37% percent of the country's population was exercising regularly, and more than 95% of the total number of students had reached the National Standards of Physical Training.

The results of the second survey of the national physique, released in September 2006, showed four major features and tendencies: First, the overall national physique had improved slightly over 2000; second, the male adult obesity rate was high, and had grown somewhat compared with the 2000 figure; third, the physique of rural residents in the age range of 20-69 was worse than that of urban residents in the same age range; and fourth, people in eastern China had better physiques than those in western China. The results of the survey of the physiques of children and young people showed that the height, weight and circumference continued to grow, and the rate of tooth disease continued to decrease, but the vital capacity of the lungs, endurance, speed, explosive force, and strength showed a tendency of decline. In addition, the numbers of overweight and obese had increased, and the rate of poor eyesight showed no change.

全运会

National Games

The National Games of the People's Republic of China, also known as the All-China Games, is the supreme sports event in

China, with delegations from each province, autonomous region, municipality and special administrative region, army, and sports association participating. It is normally held every four years. By 2005, the National Games had been held ten times, after being first hosted by Beijing from September 13 to October 3, 1959. The second games were held in Beijing from September 11 to 28, 1965; the third in Beijing from September 12 to 28, 1975; the fourth in Beijing from September 15 to 30, 1979; the fifth in Shanghai from September 18 to October 1, 1983; the sixth in Guangzhou from November 20 to December 5, 1987, with Juan Antonio Samaranch, then president of the International Olympic Committee (IOC) attending the opening ceremony; the seventh in Beijing from September 4 to 15 in 1993; the eighth in Shanghai from October 12-24 in 1997; the ninth in Guangzhou from November 11 to 25, 2001, with President Jacques Rogge of the IOC attending the opening ceremony; and the 10th in Nanjing from October 12 to 23, 2005.

The 10th National Games was a drilling of Chinese athletes who will participate in the 2008 Olympic Games in Beijing. At the 10th games, 15 athletes broke six world records 21 times; 7 hit 6 world records for 7 times; and 5 created 5 Asian records for 6 times.

少数民族运动会

Traditional Games of China's Ethnic Minorities

On the basis of the sports performances and contests held by some of China's 55 ethnic minorities in 1953, the National Traditional Games of Ethnic Minorities came into being in 1982, to protect and develop traditional minority sports culture. The games are held every four years, sponsored by the State

Mongolian wrestling

Ethnic Affairs Commission and the State Physical Culture Administration, and undertaken by local authorities. So far, they have been held eight times. Over 290 traditional minority sports have been recovered and reinvigorated. The Eighth National Traditional Games of Ethnic Minorities was hosted by Guangzhou during November 10-18, 2007. The Games consist of two categories: competitive sports and performance events. The former category includes 15 events: firework-snatching, pearl ball, wooden ball and kicking ball, shuttlecock game, dragon boat racing, swinging, crossbow shooting, top spinning, two-person tug-of-war, stilt racing, board-shoe racing, martial arts, wrestling, and horsemanship; while the latter includes more than 100 events subcategorized into competitive, technique, body-building exercise and comprehensive performances.

Among the six national games, the National Games, Intercity Games, National Games for Disabled People and University Games follow the rules of the Olympic Games, while the National Traditional Games of Ethnic Minorities and National Games for Farmers embody physical fitness, techniques, and wisdom for living and work. Participants in the National Traditional Games of Ethnic Minorities are non-professional athletes from farmers, herdsmen and fishermen to professors and urban employees; some live on the Qinghai-Tibet Plateau, while others live in primitive forests in the tropical zone. All the events, created by people of different ethnic groups, have a long history, and distinctive ethnic flavors and rich historical and cultural contents. Unlike the traditional practice, the Games have championships but no rankings or team scores.

中超联赛

China Football Association Super League

The China Football Association Super League, CSL for short, started in 2004. Developing from the previous Premier League, the CSL is the top football event in China, with a dozen or more club teams (most clubs are private) participating. About 300 million football fans in China pay close attention to the CSL, most of whom are also fans of the five European leagues; and 1,050 media organs and more than 7,000 professional sports journalists report on it. The CSL is relayed to 53 countries and regions in Asia.

The CSL adopts the system of accumulating points in home and away matches, with 28 matches for each team per season. The winner of each match gets three points, while the loser gets no points; a draw means one point each. In 2004, when the CSL was first held, the Shenzhen Jianlibao Team won the championship. In 2005, Dalian Shide won, in 2006, Shandong Luneng, and in 2007, Changchun Yatai.

CBA
CBA League

The CBA (China Basketball Association) League started in 1995, sponsored by the China Basketball Association and enrolls basketball clubs and local sports administrations. The competition season lasts from November 14 to April 23, and the games are held in the cities selected by the participating clubs and approved by the CBA ruling body.

The League includes three phases. First phase is the regular season, in which 14 teams are divided into southern and northern districts: Beijing, Liaoning, Jilin, Shandong, Henan, Shaanxi and Xinjiang in the northern district, and Shanghai, Jiangsu, Zhejiang, Fujian, Guangdong, Yunnan and Bayi in the southern district. The CBA League matches follow the home-and-away practice of four rounds in the local district and two rounds in the other district. All the teams are ranked by total scores, and the top seven are ranked in each district. Second phase is the district finals. The top four of each district in the regular season compete in rubber games home and away (the top teams in the regular season have to play one more home field match). In this way, the first, second, third and fourth prizes of each district are decided. Third phase is the playoffs. The top four teams of each district in the district finals play elimination games home and away (the top teams in the district finals have to play one more home field match). A team winning enough rounds does not have to play any more matches. The quarterfinals adopt the rubber system, while the semifinals and playoffs adopt the best-of-seven system (the defeated teams in the quarterfinals and semifinals are eliminated).

中国乒乓球超级联赛

China Table Tennis Super League

The China Table Tennis Super League (CTTSL) is the top table tennis event in China. It is sponsored by the China Table Tennis Association and China Central Television, and undertaken by the participating clubs. The games are played home and away in double rounds. Started in 1999, the CTTSL has developed into an influential event. The competition among several strong teams shows the same level and fierceness as the World Table Tennis Championships and table tennis championships in the Olympic Games.

Table tennis is considered the "national ball game" of China, which has the largest number of in-service world table tennis champions in the world. For this reason, the CTTSL attracts the best table tennis players in the world. In the 2005 CTTSL, more than 14 foreign players took part, including Timo Boll from Germany, Michael Maze from Denmark, Rye Seung-min, Oh Sang Eun and Joo Se-Hyuk from South Korea, and Koji Matsushita, Fukuhara Ai and Konishi An from Japan.

奥运理念

Three Concepts of the 2008 Olympic Games

Three concepts have been adopted for the Beijing Olympic Games, namely, Green Olympics, High-tech Olympics and People's Olympics.

Green Olympics: Environmental protection is a key prerequisite for designing and constructing the Olympic Games' facilities, while strict ecological standards and systematic guarantee systems will be established. Environmentally friendly technologies and measures will be widely applied in environmental treatment to structures and venues. Urban and rural afforestation and environmental protection will be widely enhanced in an all-round manner. Environmental awareness will be promoted among the general public, with citizens greatly encouraged to make "green" consumption choices and to actively participate in various environmental improvement activities to help improve the capital's ecological standards and build a city better fit for all to enjoy.

High-tech Olympics: A grand sporting event featuring high technology will be held by incorporating the latest domestic and international scientific and technological achievements. Beijing will upgrade its scientific innovation capabilities, boosting the industrialization of high-tech achievements and popularizing their use in daily life. The Beijing Olympic Games is to serve as a showcase for the city's high-tech achievements and innovative strength.

People's Olympics: The Beijing Olympic Games will be an occasion to spread modern Olympic ideas, while displaying China's splendid culture, Beijing's historical and cultural heritage, and its residents' positive attitudes. It will also be an opportunity to advance cultural exchanges, deepen understanding and friendship among the peoples of the world, and promote harmonious development between mankind and Nature. It will be a time to promote healthy interaction between individuals and society, and to foster mental and physical health. In line with "people-oriented" and "athletics-centered" ideas, Beijing will spare no efforts to provide quality services and build a natural and

and social environment up to the expectations of all the Games' participants.

中国印

Chinese Seal

In front of the China National Museum stands the countdown plate for the 2008 Beijing Olympic Games, with the Chinese Seal, the emblem of this Olympics, on the top.

The Olympic emblem is the most valuable intangible asset of the international Olympic Games and the core of its image, as well as the basis of Olympic market development. The various designs of the Olympic emblem are different, but all have the same five interlocking Olympic rings. They also bore patterns displaying the historical, geographical, national or cultural features of the host city or country.

The 2008 Beijing Olympic Games emblem "Chinese Seal, Dancing Beijing" was selected by the BOGOC from 1,985 entries. The emblem embodies a seal, a Chinese character and the five Olympic rings, and shows a dancing figure, signifying that Beijing enthusiastically opens its arms and welcomes friends from all over the world. The logo is a Chinese seal engraved with the Chinese character Jing (京) which means Beijing.

Dubbed "Sky, Earth and Man," the emblem of the Beijing Paralympics is a stylized figure of an athlete in motion, implying the tremendous efforts a disabled person has to make in sports as well as in life as a whole. With the unity and harmony of "sky, earth and man," the emblem incorporates Chinese characters, calligraphy and the Paralympic spirit, reflecting the Paralympic motto of "Spirit in Motion."

奥运会志愿者

Olympic Volunteers

Olympic volunteers have been busy since 2006, and will assist with the preparations for the Olympic and Paralympic Games until the closing ceremonies. The Beijing Olympic Volunteer Program comprises four projects: the "Towards the Olympics" Voluntary Service Project, the Games-time Olympic Volunteer Project, the Games-time Paralympic Volunteer Project and the Pre-Games Volunteer Project. The recruitment of Games-time volunteers was formally launched in August 2006, and ended in April 2008. There were 77,119 Games-time volunteers for the Olympic Games and about 30,000 Games-time volunteers for the Paralympic Games. The Games-time volunteers were recruited mainly in the Beijing area, mainly from among college students, as well as a certain number of residents of various provinces, compatriots from Hong Kong, Macao and Taiwan, overseas Chinese, students studying abroad and foreigners. The logo of the Beijing Olympic Volunteer Program is a combination of two interlocking heart-shaped rings, with three dancing human figures below. The two red heart-shaped rings signify that Beijing Olympic volunteers will provide heart-to-heart services to athletes, members of the "Olympic Family" and all visitors and guests, while the three dancing human figures below represent the volunteers and their devotion to the people they are to serve.

The basic requirements for Olympic volunteers are: 1) Volunteering to serve the Beijing Olympic and Paralympic games; 2) Born prior to June 29, 1990, and in good health; 3) Abiding by China's laws and regulations; 4) Able to participate in pre-Games training and related activities; 5) Able to serve for more than seven days running during the Olympic and Paralympic Games; 6) Native Chinese speakers able to communicate in at least one foreign language (applicants whose first language is not Chinese should be able to engage in conversation in Chinese); 7) Possessing the professional knowledge and skills necessary for the post.

奥运舵手
Olympic Coxswains

CCTV launched its Olympic Coxswains show in September 2006, to select coxswains for China's team in the 2008 Olympics rowing event. Any Chinese citizen aged between 18 and 60 was eligible to apply. The 80 selected contestants took part in the first season of tryouts broadcast on CCTV, with ten men and ten women chosen in February 2007 to train with the national team.

After three months of training and a second-round televised selection, two men and two women were accepted for training with the national team. Ultimately, a male and female coxswain will be chosen to compete in the 2008 Beijing Olympic Games.

福娃

Fuwa

Fuwa mascots of the 2008 Beijing Olympic Games at a shopping mall

On December 11, 2005, the official mascots of the 2008 Beijing Olympic Games — Fuwa — were unveiled. The BOCOG held a contest to solicit from around the world designs for the Beijing Olympic and Paralympic mascots from August 5, 2004 to 5:30 p.m. on December 1, 2007. The entries included

611 from China's mainland, 12 from Hong Kong, Macao and Taiwan, and 39 from foreign countries. The mascots of the Beijing Olympic Games are five little children called Fuwa. Each Fuwa has a rhyming two-syllable name — Beibei, Jingjing, Huanhuan, Yingying and Nini. When you put their names together, they compose "Bei Jing Huan Ying Ni" meaning "Welcome to Beijing." In China, the rhyming two-syllable name is a traditional way of expressing affection for children. Fuwa embody the natural characteristics of four of China's most popular animals — the Fish, the Panda, the Tibetan Antelope and the Swallow — and the Olympic Flame. The five, in different colors, also represent the Five Olympic Rings.

Beibei carries the blessing of prosperity. In China's traditional culture and art, the fish and water designs are symbols of prosperity and a bumper harvest, and people use "carp leaping through the dragon's gate" to represent one's career success and the fulfillment of one's dreams. A fish is also a symbol of surplus in Chinese culture, another measure of a good year and a good life. Strong in water sports, Beibei represents the blue Olympic ring. The designs of her head ornament are taken from water-wave designs of the New Stone Age. Jingjing, the Panda, is one of China's national treasures, symbolizing harmony between man and Nature. He represents the Black Olympic ring. The lotus designs on Jingjing's headdress were inspired by the porcelain paintings of the Song Dynasty (960-1234). Huanhuan is the big brother. He is a child of fire, symbolizing the Olympic Flame and the passion of sport. He excels at all ball games, and represents the red Olympic ring. The fiery design of his head ornament draws its inspiration from the famed Dunhuang murals. Yingying, the Tibetan Antelope, is a protected animal unique to the Qinghai-Tibet Plateau. He carries the blessing of health, and reflects Beijing's commitment to a Green Olympics.

Strong in track and field events, Yingying represents the yellow Olympic ring. His head ornament incorporates several decorative styles from the Qinghai-Tibet Plateau and Xinjiang in Western China. Nini, the Swallow, spreads good luck. Nini's figure is drawn from a kite design of Beijing's golden-winged swallow. The word swallow is pronounced "yan" in Chinese, and Yanjing is an ancient name for Beijing. Nini is strong in gymnastics and represents the green Olympic ring.

福牛乐乐

Fu Niu Lele

On September 6, 2006, the official mascot of the Beijing 2008 Paralympic Games was unveiled — an ox named Fu Niu Lele. The ox symbolizes the unremitting and staunch spirit of athletes with a disability. It dovetails with the upbeat spirit of Paralympians and the concept of "Transcendence, Equality, Integration" of the Beijing Paralympic Games. In the traditional culture of China, the ox represents good weather and bumper harvests. The design of Fu Niu Lele is based on Chinese folk engravings, New Year pictures and traditional toys.

鸟巢

The "Bird's Nest"

Dubbed the "Bird's Nest," the National Stadium is the main venue for the 2008 Beijing Olympic Games. Co-designed by the Swiss company Herzog & DeMeuron and the China Architecture Design Institute, it is a steel structure with the largest span in the world. Located in the Olympic Green Park, the "Bird's

The Bird's Nest, the main venue of the 2008 Beijing Olympic Games, under construction

Nest" covers a total area of 258,000 sq m and can accommodate 91,000 persons. It was the venue for the opening and closing ceremonies and track and field events of the 2008 Games. Construction started in December 24, 2003, and was completed by the end of 2007.

The Beijing Olympic Games included 28 sports competitions, 26 of which were held in Beijing. The Beijing Olympic Games were held in 37 venues, 31 of which are located in Beijing. The other six venues are in six co-host cities — Qingdao, Shanghai, Tianjin, Shenyang, Qinhuangdao and Hong Kong. Qingdao hosted the sailing events; Shanghai, Tianjin, Shenyang and Qinhuangdao hosted the football preliminaries; and Hong Kong hosted the equestrian events. The 31 competition venues in Beijing were used as multi-functional centers for sports, body-building, cultural and recreational activities, exhibitions, trade and commerce activities, and tourism after the Olympics.

水立方

The "Water Cube"

Dubbed the "Water Cube," the National Aquatics Center was one of the competition venues of the Beijing Olympic Games. Located in the Olympic Green Park, it covers an area of about 80,000 sq m, and has 6,000 permanent and 11,000 temporary seats. It hosted the Olympic swimming, diving, water polo and synchronized swimming events.

Inside the Olympic Green Park, there are the National Stadium, National Indoor Stadium and National Aquatics Center. In the western district of Beijing there are the Shooting Range Hall, Laoshan Velodrome and Wukesong Indoor Stadium, which were used mainly for the Olympic shooting, cycling and basketball events. The "university district" of the Games had venues at Peking University, the Beijing University of Science and Technology and other higher-education institutions. They hosted the table tennis, judo, taekwondo and other events. In the "northern scenic district" are the Shunyi Olympic Rowing-Canoeing Park, Changping Triathlon Venue and other sites, which hosted the Olympic rowing, canoe/kayak and triathlon events.

奥运村

Olympic Village

On June 26, 2005 construction started on the Beijing

Olympic Village. It was the residence for athletes and officials during the 2008 Olympic Games and Paralympic Games. The Beijing Olympic Village stands at the northern end of the north-south axis of Beijing, on which are located many cultural relics, historical sites and renowned buildings, such as the Palace Museum, Temple of Heaven and Olympic Green Park. Covering an area of 66 ha, the village is adjacent to the Olympic Green Park to the north and the cluster of Olympic venues to the south. The village is divided into residential and international quarters. The residential area had apartments, a clinic, a restaurant, a multi-functional library, an entertainment center, and a leisure and exercise quarter. The international area was the place for holding ceremonies and welcoming delegations, and other reception activities.

Covering an area of 370,000 sq m, the residential area comprises 22 six-story buildings and 20 nine-story buildings. The Olympic Village was completed at the end of 2007, and handed over to the BOCOG. It was open two weeks before the opening ceremony of the Olympic Games, and provided services for 16,000 Olympians and 7,000 Paralympians, and accompanying officials. After the two games, the village will be handed back to the proprietor company, to be transformed into a residential community. The residential apartments will be sold to the public before the Olympic Games.

强项

Competitive Events

Chinese athletes have strong competitiveness in six sports: archery, table tennis, badminton, gymnastics, diving and weightlifting. At the 2004 Athens Olympic Games, China won 32 gold medals, bringing the total number of Summer Olympic golds won by China to over 100. Chinese divers won 17, table tennis players seven, weightlifters 16, archers 14 and gymnasts 12.

After the Sydney Olympic Games in 2000, China concentrated on basic sports, including track and field, swimming and aquatics (rowing, canoe/kayak, and sailing). Since these sports involve 119 gold medals, this was called the 119 Project, aiming to make China a sporting power. The 119 gold medals available for three basic sports account for about one third of the total Olympic golds. At the Sydney Olympics, China only won one gold, for the walking race, while at the Athens Olympics, it won two for track and field, one for swimming and one for aquatics. The 119 Project sets the goal for the 2008 Olympic Games: two golds for track and field, three for swimming, and five for aquatics. At the Athens Olympics, Liu Xiang set a new world record for the 110m hurdles with a time of 12.91 seconds, becoming the first Chinese Olympic track and field gold medallist. At the same Olympics, Xing Huina won the 10,000 m race, and the unknown Sun Tiantian and Li Ting won the gold for women's doubles of tennis.

体彩

Sports Lottery

In 1989 China instituted its first sports lottery, to raise funds for the 11th Asian Games. In 1994 the Sports Lottery Management Center under the State Administration of Physical Culture was established, with branch offices in provinces and cities nationwide, following international practices. The lottery raised 121.7 billion yuan from 1994 to 2005, raising nearly 40 billion yuan for sports after the deduction of 50% refund and 15%

distribution fee. In 2006, sales reached 32.2 billion yuan, raising 10.66 billion yuan for sports.

Winners of up to 10,000 yuan are exempt from income tax, and winners of more than that amount are taxed at the rate of 20%. Besides sports, money raised by the sports lottery is used for social welfare, Red Cross projects, the construction and maintenance of recreational and educational venues for children, the 2008 Beijing Olympic Games, the disabled, rural medical aid and the Nationwide Physical Fitness Program.

Community exercise equipments are financially supported by the sports lottery welfare fund.

图书在版编目（CIP）数据

关键词读中国：英文 / 夏和文编.
北京：外文出版社，2008年
ISBN 978-7-119-05347-9
Ⅰ.关… Ⅱ.夏… Ⅲ.中国—概况—英文 Ⅳ.K92
中国版本图书馆CIP数据核字（2008）第061668号

企　　划：黄友义　李振国
主　　编：呼宝民
文字编辑：夏和文
中文改稿：王传民
封面设计：北京端直世纪广告有限公司
英文翻译：李 洋　王 琴　冯 鑫　曲 磊　周晓刚　严 晶
英文审定：Paul White　贺 军　徐明强
内文设计：李 耀
印刷监制：张国祥

关键词读中国
夏和文

出版发行：
外文出版社（中国北京百万庄大街24号）
邮政编码：　100037
网址：http://www.flp.com.cn
电话：008610-68320579（总编室）
　　　008610-68995852（发行部）
　　　008610-68327750（版权部）
印刷：北京外文印刷厂
开本：150mm×230mm　　1/16　　印张：17.75
2008年第1版第1次印刷
　　　（英）
ISBN 978-7-119-05347-9
　　　06000（平）
　　　17-E-3806P
